The Mood of America
A Journey Toward Liberty

By James F. McCarty and Jim Borgman

With forewords by
John P. Zanotti and George R. Blake

Design by
Ron Huff, Elmer Wetenkamp
and Bob Kinney

Edited by
Cindy Holm and Jim Dean

THE CINCINNATI ENQUIRER

Congratulations Kitty! Perhaps this can help you sort out the best locations!

Published by

The Cincinnati Enquirer
617 Vine Street
Cincinnati, Ohio 45202

Copyright © 1986 The Cincinnati Enquirer
No part of this book may be reproduced in any form or by any means without the prior, written permission of the publisher, excluding brief excerpts within reviews written specifically for inclusion in a magazine or newspaper.

Library of Congress Catalog Card Number 86-072051, *ISBN: 0-9609632-3-5*

Printed by The Merten Company, Cincinnati, Ohio.

A Word from the Publisher

And now the book.

Our readers told us they loved the work of Jim McCarty and Jim Borgman as they traveled across the USA toward the Statue of Liberty celebrations. They told us they wanted more.

We knew that all the work from their travels was not published. Borgman cartoons and McCarty stories were available to add something new and special to a book. So here we are.

All of us at *The Cincinnati Enquirer* were proud of this series of stories and drawings, which appeared June 15 through July 6, 1986. Borgman and McCarty proved we were correct to send them on the road.

Borgman joined *The Enquirer* in June, 1976. The day after his 10th anniversary here, he stepped on a plane to begin chronicling the mood of America.

In 1976, he was a young graduate of Kenyon College seeking a job as an editorial cartoonist. How much would *The Enquirer* need to pay him? "Whatever is offered," he said on his initial job application. Jim Borgman wanted to work in his home town.

In 1986, he is one of America's best-known cartoonists. His work is syndicated in more than 200 newspapers, and he has won many awards for journalistic excellence. He constantly makes us proud.

McCarty is a relative newcomer to *The Enquirer*, having joined us in March, 1985, from the *Columbus Citizen-Journal*.

He grew up in Akron and graduated from the University of Akron in 1977. His journalism career took him to Santa Monica (Calif.), Akron, Medina (Ohio) and York (Pa.) before Columbus, where he started in 1983.

After joining *The Enquirer* Metro staff last year, McCarty quickly proved he was a top reporter and writer.

The Borgman-McCarty collaboration on this project brought our readers a memorable series/ We hope this book preserves those memories.

Enjoy it.

—John P. Zanotti
President and Publisher
The Cincinnati Enquirer

P.S. Suzanne McCarty and Lynn Borgman deserve a special thanks. The two Jims were away from home for 27 straight days, but their wives were supportive of all aspects of this journey. We were pleased that Suzanne and Lynn so willingly shared these two special journalists with our readers.

A Word from the Editor

The trip was a journalist's dream.

We all like to lean back in our chairs and think about the perfect assignment. This, perhaps, was it. Jim Borgman and Jim McCarty were sent on the road with a single mission: Travel across America and tell us what people are thinking and doing.

Their arrival in Seattle in early June followed many weeks of planning. An itinerary had been carefully mapped out.

They could change their minds. If they discovered a more interesting story in another town, Borgman and McCarty had instant authorization to go there.

Only one destination was certain. The whole trip was aimed at their arrival in New York City in time for the celebration of the 100th anniversary of the Statue of Liberty. The lighting ceremony was July 3 and the parade of the tall ships July 4. A weekend full of festivities would follow.

Before Borgman and McCarty left Cincinnati, we chose a name for their project: "The Mood of America '86: A Journey Toward Liberty."

That name became part of their goal: to assess the country's mood. But we made it clear to the two journeying journalists that "mood" didn't mean political mood. Or economic mood. We didn't want them asking everyone what they thought of Ronald Reagan or the nation's economy.

We wanted mood to mean what people think about where they lived and how they lived. We wanted our readers to feel the varying personalities of America.

I was proud of the job they did. During the 3½ weeks their work appeared in *The Cincinnati Enquirer*, they created an excitement felt throughout the community. Readers were eager for the next report. They enjoyed McCarty's writings and Borgman's drawings.

Their editor enjoyed the work, too. There was some personal satisfaction involved.

Most great newspaper ideas are generated by reporters, not editors. The reporter, whether on the "beat" at city hall or in the constant search of interesting topics to write about, tells the editor about an idea. The editor approves or modifies or disapproves.

In this case, the idea came from the editor. I joined millions of Americans in looking forward to the Statue of Liberty celebrations. I wanted to be sure that *The Enquirer* provided some special coverage. I wondered how.

The idea came to me to put a reporter on the road, journeying toward Liberty. I chose Jim McCarty because I thought his writing ability would give this assignment the special touch I was seeking.

I then started wondering how to illustrate the stories. At first I planned to send a photographer. Then I thought about sending Jim Borgman, and the light bulb grew brighter. Borgman was a natural for this one. His artistic talents and his ability to offer readers extraordinary insights would make the project better.

Both McCarty and Borgman liked the idea immediately, although Borgman said he wouldn't commit to it until speaking with his wife, Lynn. "She told me that if I *didn't* go, she'd divorce me," he said the next morning.

Lynn, who helped publish this book, knew what everyone in our newsroom knew: This *was* the dream assignment.

I expected it also to be a bit of a nightmare. I didn't know whether the two Jims would become friends or enemies as they traveled. I didn't know how they would find time for little things like laundry. I didn't know whether they could work together — whether Borgman would insist that McCarty's words expand on the stories being told in the drawings or whether McCarty would insist that Borgman merely illustrate the stories.

They had to find ways not only to work together, but to live together. To chase planes. To share hotel rooms and rental cars and meals. To adjust to each other's schedules for sleeping and eating and writing and drawing.

I told them to learn to have fun. It wouldn't always be easy, but their moments of enjoyment would show up in their work.

Without doubt, they did have fun. And our readers enjoyed the trip along with them. As did this editor, readers wanted more. We're pleased to bring you this expanded version of the "Journey Toward Liberty."

— George R. Blake
Editor and Vice President
The Cincinnati Enquirer

The Cincinnati Enquirer wishes to acknowledge the time, talent and teamwork of the employees involved in producing *The Mood of America* as both a newspaper series and a book.

Introduction

At first, neither of us knew the other well enough to know that each was in a rut.

For 10 years, editorial cartoonist Jim Borgman had drawn a daily dose of the timely, rib-tickling political humor that earned him a reputation as one of the best in the business. He rarely escaped the sanctum of his third floor office at *The Cincinnati Enquirer*, however, and lately he suspected a few kinks had developed in his creativity.

I had worked general assignment out of the *Enquirer's* fourth-floor Metro department for a year, but already the routine of reporting city hall, going on police and fire runs and making late-night phone calls to ungrateful politicians and grieving widows had become tedious.

Both of us were ripe for a change when our editor, George Blake, offered us the assignment of a lifetime, a "plum" in the lingo of the business.

"Just go out there and have fun," Blake urged. "If you're enjoying yourselves, your readers will enjoy themselves." At least that was what we thought he said.

The concept was unique: team a reporter with a cartoonist, their only instructions being to travel to exotic places, observe breathtaking sights, interview interesting people, follow their noses and generally have a good time criss-crossing the continent at the company's expense. We could write and draw whatever we pleased in chronicling the mood of America.

What hungry journalists wouldn't jump at the chance? We were the envy of friends, co-workers and peers, all of whom thought we were embarking on a relaxing monthlong journey to vacationland. They couldn't have been more wrong.

We worked for a month without a day off. Some mornings we awoke at 5:30 a.m. to catch an early flight; some nights we worked until 2 a.m. to finish stories or illustrations. It was a grueling schedule — 15 separate stops from June 9 to July 5.

We lived out of suitcases, traveling with only a couple of changes of clothes. We often grabbed meals on the run, sometimes while driving like racers to catch a plane or reach a story location, other times while being jostled by turbulence 30,000 feet in the air. We worked in cars, airplanes, hotel lobbies, airports, parks and restaurants.

Recreation? We dove into two pools, and the water in one, in Sun City, Ariz., must have been 90 degrees. We swam at a grand total of one beach — at the Great Salt Lake. More about that later.

But what a wonderful month, never knowing from one day to the next what sort of strange characters we would encounter, what new episode lay over the horizon, what acts of nature might stand in our way. We had no scheduled interviews or story demands, only ideas, hopes and expectations.

Often our editors didn't know where we were or what we were doing. But how could we solve these mysteries for them when we didn't know the answers ourselves? We thought this approach kept the series fresh; the editors pulled their hair out and kept their fingers crossed.

No doubt about it, the series could have bombed. Fortunately, we never had to call in to report, "Sorry, we don't have anything to write about today." We constantly were amazed at the dumb luck we had finding interesting people at each stop along the way.

Of course, the further potential for disaster always lurked in the back of our minds. Like, what if we didn't get along and spent our days fighting and arguing? What if we missed a flight? One of us came down sick? Wrecked a car? Missed a deadline? Luckily, none of those trip-wrecking tragedies occurred.

Actually, we thought we made a pretty good team. Often during the course of one of my interviews, Borgman would join in with excellent questions. Too bad I couldn't reciprocate by pitching in on some of his sketches.

Being on our own, we became each other's most valued critic. We knew something special was happening, that our work was capturing the flavor of our experiences even if we couldn't see our finished products in *The Enquirer*. In the evening, when we took a break to relax and eat, we usually reflected on the day and gave ourselves a much-needed pat on the back. Another day had passed, and it was working just as we had hoped it would.

What follows are not hard news stories that broke before our eyes at each whistle stop. These stories are simple accounts drawn from the lives of ordinary people. We found that regular people usually have the best stories to tell.

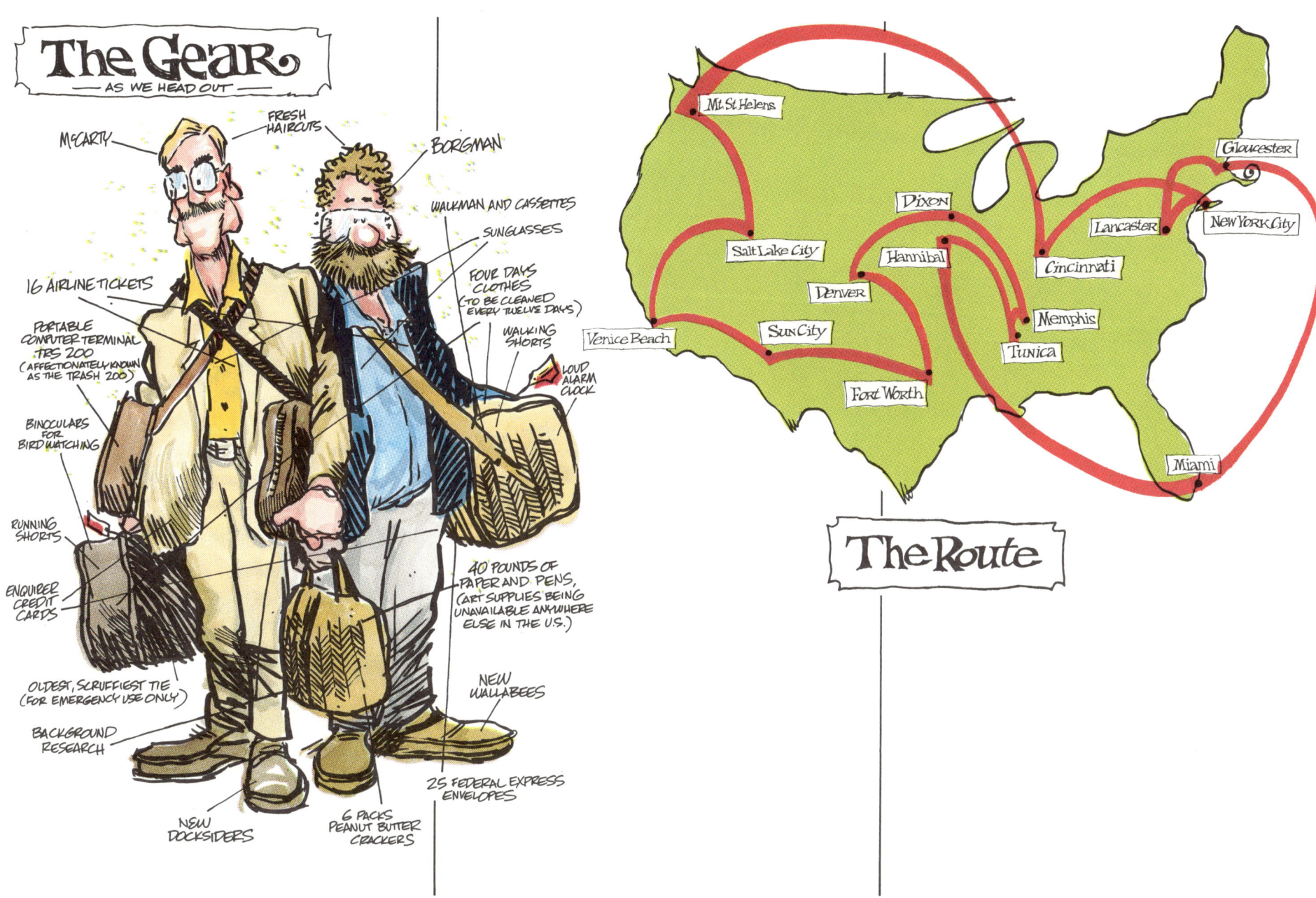

The Mood of

America

Before the mountain blew, and more so in the years since, the media made Harry Truman a folk hero.

People everywhere could embrace Truman's grizzled, weather-worn face as a lovable, eccentric old uncle's. Many anguished over his certain fate in the foreboding days of spring, 1980, when magnificent, snow-capped Mount St. Helens rumbled and gushed steam as a harbinger of its eruption.

"If it's gonna take me, let it come and get me," Truman had challenged the mountain defiantly. "That damn mountain doesn't dare blow up on me."

In his mind, he was invincible. Such are the ingredients of legends.

The 83-year-old codger with the famous name said he had a hiding hole beneath his Mount St. Helens lodge where he planned to safeguard himself, his 16 cats and a barrel of whiskey.

He never had a chance. It is generally accepted that Truman, his cats and his whiskey are buried beneath 300 feet of mud and water. No trace of Truman or his lodge has ever been found.

The public's fascination with Truman continues in the aftermath of the worst volcanic eruption in North American history. Today, at a barren bluff overlooking the gaping, mile-wide hole that once was Mount St. Helens, it is Truman's name that is most often spoken by the carloads of curious tourists. The site of his last stand on the banks of Spirit Lake provides visitors a telling panorama of the volcano's destruction.

Truman prophesied just such a scene. "If she does blow," he said, "people will come up the road and see a mountain of lava, and they'll say, 'Harry Truman is under there.'"

Most outsiders admire Truman's courageous stand. But a few local people say he was just plain dumb.

Royal Andrews is one who doesn't remember Truman in a heroic light. Andrews, every bit the colorful character that Truman was, operates a roadside motel in Packwood about 30 miles from Spirit Lake in the Cascade Mountains. He's tall and still tough from his days as a lumberjack; he has tattoos on both arms from his days as a merchant marine and wears a pencil-thin gray mustache. He claims to drink half a case of Buckhorn beer a night. "I have every night for 40 years, no sense stopping now," drawled Andrews, who's in his 60s.

Andrews was working as a lumberjack when he had his first and worst run-in with Truman. It happened about 18 years ago, which demonstrates how long old Washington mountain men can carry a grudge.

Andrews was supervising a team of loggers at the

EXPERIENCING MT. ST. HELENS HAS A LOT TO DO WITH COLOR. THE GREENS, BLUES AND YELLOWS OF THE MILES OF FERNS AND DOUGLAS FIRS END SUDDENLY IN THE ASHEN COLORLESSNESS OF THE DEVASTATED AREA, ALL AGAINST A BLINDING BLUE SKY.

time. At the end of a long day of cutting 200-foot Douglas firs, the crew, as loggers are apt to do, headed for the nearest tavern, which happened to be Truman's Mount St. Helens Lodge.

All were in a jovial mood. Andrews and his loggers were swilling bottles of cold Olympia beer, and Truman kept setting them up with fresh rounds at 50 cents a bottle. But when it came time for Andrews to ▶

ROYAL AND BERTHA ANDREWS
OWNERS OF THE ROYAL INN, PACKWOOD, WASHINGTON
(POP. 1000)

ROYAL REMEMBERS MT. ST. HELENS' LEGENDARY HARRY TRUMAN AS 'AN OLD COOT' WHO HAD CHARGED HIM HIGH PRICES FOR BEER AT HIS SPIRIT LAKE LODGE

BERTHA HAS LIVED 21 YEARS AT THE FOOT OF A MOUNTAIN WHOSE NAME SHE HAD NEVER THOUGHT TO ASK.

buy a round, Truman charged $1 a bottle.

"I asked Harry, 'What the hell you doing here?' And he said, 'Those guys have to work for a living. You don't,'" Andrews said, shaking his head in disbelief nearly two decades later.

"He sure was a cantankerous old goat. I never did like him anyway. He got what he deserved," Andrews said. "I don't think he was a brave hero like people are making him out to be today. If you ask me, he just didn't think the mountain was gonna do what it did."

Andrews' face doesn't match his words: He is grinning and sipping coffee from a mug constructed of Mount St. Helens ash. He shakes out the last few drops of coffee into the grass, and the mug's handle breaks off in his hand. Despite his protests and bold proclamations, it is apparent that Andrews really liked Truman.

Truman, of course, isn't available to comment on Andrews' claims. But his legendary life remains intact despite current detractors.

Some older residents still remember how, for more than 50 summers, Truman played the piano for the legions of young campers who came to fish and swim in Spirit Lake's crystal-clear waters. And how, during the winters, he sat on the same piano stool serenading hunters and loggers who were attracted to the mountain wilderness. Former Supreme Court Justice William O. Douglas was a friend of Truman's and a frequent visitor to the lodge.

Such a life was too good for Truman to give up at his age, never mind those government scientists and forest service workers who told him the mountain could blow up any time.

On the morning of May 18, 1980, the predictions

PACKWOOD, WASHINGTON / IN THE SHADOW OF TATOOSH AND SNOW-COVERED MT. RAINIER

12 WASHINGTON

were fulfilled. Andrews and his wife of 28 years, Bertha, speak of an incredible sight. There were booms and explosions from earthquakes, and the sounds from the volcano intermingled with claps of thunder from a storm that was spawned in the thick mushroom clouds of black ash billowing high into the sky.

"I'd even call it beautiful before it got here. It was translucent with the sunlight shining from behind the cloud," Bertha Andrews said.

The ash cloud headed straight toward Packwood.

First came a hail of pebbles and small rocks raining down on rooftops — pieces of the mountain, actually, jettisoned by the force of the volcano's blast. Then, as the cloud passed over head, six inches of fine ash settled onto everything in sight.

The midday sky turned as black as a moonless night, and life from Packwood to Seattle, 100 miles north, choked to a halt. Some people panicked; a few tried futilely to leave in their cars. One woman thought she was witnessing the end of the world, Bertha Andrews said.

Little evidence of the spectacle remains outside the blast zone today. But inside the 150 square miles of forest devastated by the volcano, little has changed.

As far as the eye can see, once towering firs, pine and hemlock lie like symmetrical match sticks on the bare ground, uprooted or snapped at their bases. Not a single tree within 10 miles of the mountain withstood the blast of superheated, volcanic gases with the explosive equivalent of a 24-megaton nuclear bomb.

On a hill by the roadside, a single, rusty old car sits on its belly — a monument to how the volcano dealt with man-made objects. It belonged to the Parker family whose three members died at a mining camp near the volcano. The crumpled Grand Prix was blown across the road, sandblasted and stripped of all its paint, upholstery and plastic trim.

Deep in the valley between Mount St. Helens and Windy Ridge — at five miles, the closest accessible site to the volcano — lies a new Spirit Lake, much wider and deeper than its predecessor. Much of its surface is covered by stripped logs, floating and rotting.

On the north side of the lake, under 300 feet of mud and water is where Truman's lodge once stood as inviting as a picture post card.

North of the lake is the mountain, or what is left of it. The peak, once as majestic as the nearby 14,400-foot Mount Rainier, is now a crumbled shell. A huge gaping crater still spits and billows steam from its guts. The contour of its sides resembles the barren, pockmarked surface of the moon.

A POWERFUL MEMORIAL IN THE MIDST OF THE DESOLATED MILES IS THIS FENCED-OFF CAR, UNDISTURBED SINCE IT WAS HURLED ACROSS THE ROAD ON MAY 18, 1980, BY THE ERUPTION. NONE OF ITS PLASTIC, RUBBER, GLASS, PAINT OR VINYL SURVIVED THE 300 MPH HEAT BLAST. IT IS 10 MILES FROM THE MOUNTAIN.

The scene from Windy Ridge offers thrill-seekers a vista of the region. It is an ugly, albeit breathtaking, view.

Reaching Windy Ridge requires a drive of 16 miles on a dusty, one-lane road with no guardrails to protect cars from the steep drops. But only there can a visitor see close-up the massive destruction of the volcano and the slow, gradual recovery.

Small tufts of weeds and bunches of huckleberry bushes have begun to sprout from crevices in the sun-bleached lava. Mountain bluebirds and pocket gophers are venturing back into the harsh environment.

Life will be allowed to regenerate naturally in the devastated zone, where the government has set aside 110,000 acres as a national monument. Scientists expect a century will pass before the recovery is complete.

One wonders if perhaps Truman foresaw what was in store for his beautiful lake and mountain, and for that reason chose to join 56 others as a martyr to the volcano. ▶

WASHINGTON 13

MT. ST. HELENS FROM NEAREST ACCESSIBLE MOUNTAINSIDE, WINDY RIDGE

"What would I do?" Truman wondered in the days preceding his death. "I can't leave this place. If the mountain wants to take me down that hill feet first, let her try. I'm not going.

"People just say I'm stubborn and bullheaded. I'd die down there being away from this place, away from my cats and birds."

Perhaps Truman looked into the future and found death preferable to life on the highway with its endless stream of logging trucks and its tourist traps sprouting like weeds to sell shelves full of paper weights and pens and coffee mugs, all made from Mount St. Helens ash.

Perhaps Truman feared he would end up like old Critch, a bachelor storekeeper who became a paranoid hermit after the volcano blew and who refused to touch a book about the mountain presented to him as a gift by Bertha Andrews.

In Truman's mind, Spirit Lake and Mount St. Helens will always remain as they were before the eruption — gorgeous and serene. ■

Salt Lake City, Utah

JIM BORGMAN
SALT LAKE CITY GENEALOGICAL LIBRARY

At the end of another day spent poring over reels of microfilm, reams of books and piles of documents, Max and Eva Whitaker relax in the shade of a sycamore outside the massive Genealogical Library at Temple Square. They are in no hurry to get home and have no qualms about delivering a short personal history lesson to a couple of strangers from Cincinnati.

A Whitaker marched into Britain with the army of William the Conqueror, they said. An ancestor to be proud of, you say? Further research found that the noble warrior "took advantage of women."

Eva's family, the Brownfields, on the other hand, were a more sedate clan with only minor scandals to conceal. Mild stuff such as a great-grandmother who was denied admission into the Daughters of the American Revolution for "fudging" some important dates.

Max and Eva Whitaker have spent their lives charting their family tree. Their mission is rooted among the primary tenets of their religion — that the living are obligated to do all they can to save the souls of their dead relatives.

The Whitakers are Mormons, members of the Church of Jesus Christ of Latter-day Saints, which is based in Salt Lake City and whose members make up 60% of the city's population.

For the Whitakers, as with all 3.6 million members of the Mormon Church, building a family tree is not a whimsical project. It is a responsibility in life. To save your ancestors, you must identify them.

"We believe the family is eternal, that life together can be continued beyond the grave," said Whitaker, 67, a tall, gray-haired man eager to proselytize. "It is our duty to our relatives to do their work by proxy. Our work can mean salvation for our dead ancestors."

There is no better place to conduct an ancestral study than at the Genealogical Library, a modern four-story granite building that contains the names of 88 million deceased people. It is free and open to the public and has a staff of 200 volunteers who answer questions and help guide searches.

Its aisles are lined with untold volumes and filled with a cross-section of people from around the world who have come with a single purpose — to find their roots.

WE'VE SEEN THREE DISTINCT GROUPS OF PEOPLE IN THE SALT LAKE CITY AREA:

— THE OLD-WEST HOLDOVER —
THERE'S A HOT-SUN, BLEACHED-CONCRETE, AUTHENTIC-WESTERN-OUTPOST FEELING ON THE STREETS HERE, AND SOME CHARACTERS WHO APPEAR TO HAVE SURVIVED THE 1850s.

The library has records from practically every country: birth, marriage, death and probate records, census returns, parish registers, passenger lists of immigrants, military records, deeds, land grants, cemetery records and family histories.

There are volumes of family geneaologies, periodicals, histories of towns, counties and states, too. A quick check finds a 1930-31 city directory for Norwood, a 1926 book of *Cincinnati's Colored Citizens* and numerous Cincinnati and Southwest Ohio directories and reference books.

Anyone who has explored a family tree knows that no one descends entirely from saints. A family history inevitably shakes some skeletons from the closet.

"Skeletons? You bet," says Eva Whitaker with a mischievous gleam in her eyes. She is a former county clerk in her mid-60s with pure white hair and a ready grin.

"The more you get into it, the more you learn to accept what you find," she says.

Although the Whitakers have traced Max's family back to British royalty, they only recently learned that his stepmother, who is still alive, is 10 years older than she claims. When she married Max's father, she said she was 21. In fact, she was 31.

"When she reached Social Security age, she had to do some repenting, and I'm sure, some explaining, too," Eva Whitaker said.

The couple is proud of Max's great-grandfather, George Whitaker, who came to Salt Lake City in 1847 with the original group of Mormon settlers led by Brigham Young. It was Whitaker who baked the adobe bricks in the wall that surrounds Temple Square,

— THE MORMONS —
THESE FOLKS HAVE BEEN EXCEEDINGLY KIND. ALMOST MADDENINGLY KIND. THEY ARE CREASELESS, SUBURBAN, OSMONDLY STRAIGHT. THEY WAX THEIR DRIVEWAYS. THEY IRON THEIR LAWNS. THEY HAVE A SPIC-AND-SPAN CITY TO SHOW FOR IT.

— THE ENVIRONMENTALISTS —
YOU FIND THEM RIDING THEIR BIKES UP MOUNTAINS WITH NO SHIRTS. THEY ARE FILLING THEIR CANTEENS IN BROOKS. THEY SELDOM COME DOWN INTO THE CITY.

which is situated on 10 acres in the heart of the city.

Eva Whitaker hasn't found any royalty in her blood, but a research specialist has spoken of "the integrity of her relatives." They include a bright school teacher who lived in Germany during the early 1800s and a pair of Missouri brothers who fought for the Union during the Civil War and died in a prisoner-of-war camp at Andersonville, Ga.

Some of the Whitakers' discoveries have been so unlikely and amazing that they believe their search is guided by divine providence.

"This is the spirit of Elijah working within us," Eva Whitaker said.

Indeed, constructing a family tree is an arduous task when a single great-great-grandfather can have more than 1,000 descendants. The Genealogical Library, the largest of its kind in the world, makes the search possible. ■

Utah Sketchbook
by Jim Borgman

The 'This is the Place' monument grandly commemorates Brigham Young's first words upon leading the Mormons into the Salt Lake Valley.

For all their significance to Mormon history, the words seem too casual for such epic treatment, don't they?....

What if Neil Armstrong had stepped onto the moon and said, 'So, what time is lunch?' Would we have highway signs pointing to the 'Who Gets The Pastrami On Rye?' monument?

Lost among their many efforts in redemption, the people of Utah have single-handedly saved the dying leisure suit industry.

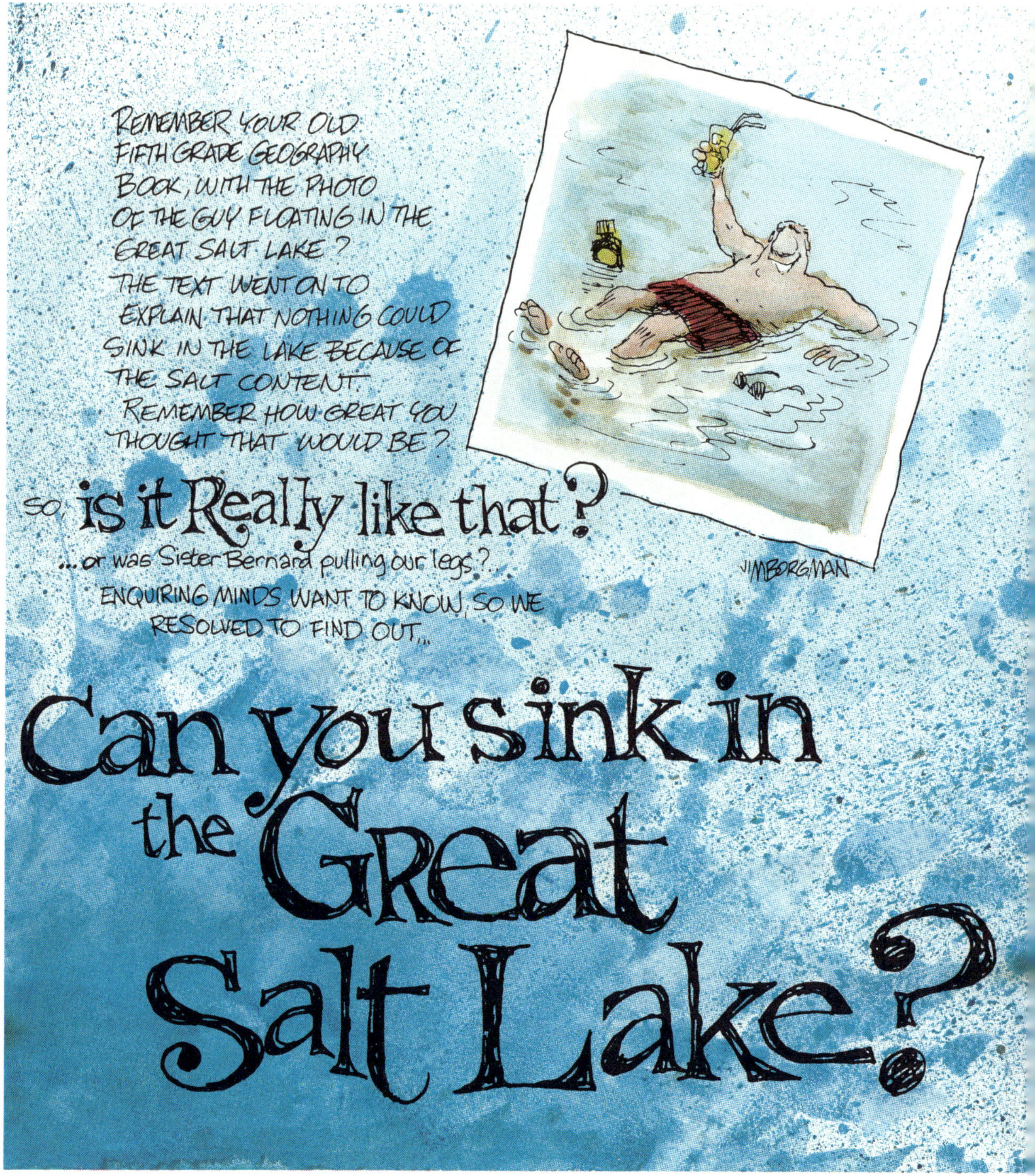

A conviction we both held for nearly a lifetime was dashed today.

We came to Salt Lake City with a common purpose. Just like that jolly fellow pictured in our grammar school geography books, we envisioned ourselves laughing and splashing in the briny waters of the Great Salt Lake as buoyant as bobbers on a fishing line.

What a joy it would be to glide effortlessly across the tranquil water without a worry in the world. It's impossible to sink in the Great Salt Lake, and there are no records of a swimmer ever drowning there. But what a shock we were in for.

The first sign that our dream bubble might be popped came when, despite frequent questioning, we found that most area residents we spoke to didn't know where to find the Great Salt Lake's beaches, and none had ever had the courage to swim there. We apparently were more likely to find bathers in the Ohio River at the mouth of Mill Creek than at this national landmark.

The Great Salt Lake, a huge inland sea that is six times saltier than the ocean, once was a popular tourist attraction in the West. But rising waters the last 20 years submerged many of its best beaches. Even without the floods, raw sewage and industrial waste dumped into the lake made swimming a risky sport.

Undaunted, we learned that a beach was still open on Willard Bay about an hour's drive north near Ogden. We set off.

The appearance of the lake at Willard Bay gave us no indication of what to expect. Only the picturesque Wasatch Mountains that lined its western shore

Remember your old fifth grade geography book, with the photo of the guy floating in the Great Salt Lake? The text went on to explain that nothing could sink in the lake because of the salt content. Remember how great you thought that would be?

So, is it Really like that?
...or was Sister Bernard pulling our legs?
Enquiring minds want to know, so we resolved to find out...

Can you sink in the Great Salt Lake?

—JIM BORGMAN

20 UTAH

Answer:

OF COURSE YOU CAN. EVEN THOUGH WE'RE AMATEURS WE WERE ABLE TO DO IT IMMEDIATELY. IN FACT, IT TOOK SOME DOING TO FLOAT AT ALL. IT PROVED TO BE NO BIG SHAKES TO REMAIN ENTIRELY SUBMERGED FOR MINUTES AT A TIME, AND EVEN THE FISH SEEMED TO BE STRUGGLING TO KEEP OFF THE BOTTOM.

BEFORE LONG WE WERE WONDERING IF ANYTHING WOULD FLOAT AND BEGAN EXPERIMENTING.....

	Float	Sort of Float	Sink
BORGMAN/McCARTY	☐	✓	☐
INFLATED BEACH BALL	☐	✓	☐
VENUS DRAWING PENCIL (2B)	☐	☐	✓
SUNGLASSES	☐	☐	✓
1 PAIR WALLABEES	☐	☐	✓
RAND McNALLY 1986 ROAD ATLAS	☐	✓	☐
PORTABLE COMPUTER TERMINAL TRS 200	☐	☐	✓

......SO, IF SISTER BERNARD WAS LYING TO US ABOUT THE Great Salt Lake, (and we already know she was lying to us about coffee being the main crop in Colombia,) THEN WHAT DO YOU SUPPOSE THE FIFTY STATE CAPITALS REALLY ARE?

---

distinguished it from any other lake. And other swimmers were there — a good sign.

Stepping tentatively into the cold water, our expectations rose. We tried to ignore the scum on the water surface, the gnats swarming around our heads and the squirming, maggot-like larvae paddling nearby. Try as we might, however, it was impossible not to notice the school of trophy-sized carp engaged in a frenzy within splashing distance of our legs.

We persevered. Our excitement rose in anticipation. Yes, I said, I *do* feel a buoyancy in my legs. You're right, said Borgman, I can *smell* the salt in the air.

Then, in unison, we dropped into the water . . . and sunk like stones.

What's going on here? We were incredulous. Did someone give us bad directions? I risked dipping my tongue into the water. Not a trace of salt.

John Hall of Ogden, who works for the park service at Willard Bay, had an explanation. A huge man-made dike spans the mouth of the bay where it meets the lake, he said, which keeps the salt water in the lake from mingling with the fresh water in the stream-fed bay. Otherwise, no one would want to swim, boat or fish in the bay, he said.

"I've lived here my whole life, and I've never been in the Great Salt Lake," said Hall, 18. "In fact, I can't say I know anyone who has. The lake's pretty gunky. I don't know why anyone would want to swim in it."

I protested. What about the pictures of people in geography books floating effortlessly on their backs, a drink in one hand, a book in the other?

"That was years ago" was Hall's curt explanation.

At the risk of showing my age, I dropped the argument.

But I wondered what type of misleading photographs geography books today are using to illustrate the Great Salt Lake. Do they show carp, gnats and industrial waste driving swimmers from its waters? Or are students still being led astray? ∎

Venice Beach, California

IF CALIFORNIA IS A CARICATURE OF AMERICA, VENICE BEACH IS THE CARICATURE OF CALIFORNIA.....

JIM BORGMAN

Every eye on the Venice Beach boardwalk must have been on him at one time or another, you could hardly miss him, this proud strutting peacock of a man with earphones pinned on his head and a cigarette stuck between his lips.

He swaggered by admiring girls on roller skates, winked at a woman in a bikini and acknowledged a whistle with a wave of his hand.

The Splatter Man, a.k.a. the Hollywood Indian, a.k.a. Mr. Fantasy, was back in town with a new look and a new found freedom, and he planned to milk the moment for all it was worth.

"I lost my relationship just yesterday, but that's cool," said the man of many monikers whose given name — Ron Perosi — he prefers not to use. "That's why I came to California, to hang out and be freaky like this. That's why I'm down here today, to check out the sun, ogle the chicks, freak people out, check out their reactions, that sort of thing."

People stare at Perosi and whisper as they pass by. It is Perosi's appearance, not his popularity, that accounts for the attention he attracts during his boardwalk promenade.

Perosi felt he had to shake up his life a little after the breakup with his girlfriend. He started by having his jet-black hair cut in a Mohawk, which he complemented with a checkerboard cut on the sides. Then, at the risk of blending into the crowd, he bleached his black hair blond and tinted it every color of the rainbow.

Perosi enhanced his eye-catching hairdo by splattering multicolored paint on his jeans and T-shirt — hence the Splatter Man.

"Pretty soon I'll be a star. Look for me, man," he said as he split for no particular destination — just wherever he could flaunt his looks and relish the attention.

Perosi, a native of Oklahoma City who boasts of being half Cherokee Indian, said he makes a living working behind the camera. He stepped in front of the camera recently, however, when a friend cast him in the lead of a movie called *Mr. Fantasy*. He plays a Hollywood designer in the movie, from which he derives his other two nicknames.

Perosi may stand out in a crowd, but he's far from

being the sole contributor to Venice Beach's reputation as a haven for some of the most eccentric characters on earth. Any given day on this 10-block stretch of coastline, which separates the fashionable enclaves of Santa Monica and Marina del Rey, convicts mingle with professors, millionaires deal with derelicts, body builders converse with mental midgets — all in front of a varied backdrop of singers, dancers, jugglers and park bench prophets.

All have a place in the surf hierarchy. Some fit the bill for Southern California coolness better than others. The "cool" sport tanned, well-muscled physiques, cropped hairdos, Jam shorts that stretch well below the knees, stereo earphones and, of course, shades.

Most important, however, is having a sport that can help you show off and call attention to yourself. For most this means jogging, biking, walking with hand weights, roller skating, skate boarding, playing paddle ball, basketball or volleyball, pumping iron in "the pit" or practicing the ancient arts of tai chi, karate, kung fu, boxing or pickpocketing.

Anyone who simply strolls the boardwalk and stares marks himself as a tourist.

Venice has a plethora of sidewalk vendors and storefront merchants who cater to zany clientele. A sign welcomes all to the "Eternal Venice Beach Carnival." This beachfront agora is probably the closest thing this megalopolis — or any city west of New York — has to an Asian bazaar. And yes, it is bizarre.

"It used to be that nice people would come down here with better culture. But now on the weekends, whew, it's like a circus," said Bob Iglesias, who relaxes on the Venice Pier with a pole in the water and an anchovy on a hook.

Iglesias pauses to lament two large flounder that have escaped his line the last few minutes. He pays no mind to the signs posted on piers all down the coast that warn: "Don't eat the white croaker, also known as kingfish and tomcod, common in these waters. ▶

VENICE BEACH, CALIFORNIA

CALIFORNIA 25

Specimens have been found by the state Department of Health Services to contain trace amounts of DDT and PCBs."

"Yeah, it gets crazy in Venice now, like a zoo with people playing guitars all the time. I saw a guy juggling running chain saws a week ago. During the Olympics with the Europeans down here, whoa, it was like a nude beach," says Iglesias, who answers the obvious question before it is asked — no, he isn't related to Julio. But this Iglesias is not wanting for good looks, either. He is slim with thick salt-and-pepper hair and wears a pair of dark shades on his well-tanned face.

"The movie stars, the beautiful people, they don't come out here any more. They go out there," he says, pointing south in the direction of Marina del Rey.

No matter, Iglesias says. He expects to be off this pier, out of Venice and on a yacht in a couple of years anyway. He has a formula for a special laundry process, see, that binds scents to a washer load's rinse cycle. He claims that Procter and Gamble offered him $50,000 for the marketing rights to the secret formula. But he turned down the offer — not big enough, he said.

"Right now, I figure I'm sitting on $20 million with this thing. Like someone told me the other day, 999 people are going to turn me down for the kind of money I want. But there's that one person who won't, and that's who I'm looking for," he said dreamily, reeling in his line. No fish, no bait.

"I'd like to develop a new camera, too, one that I could drop down the line to see when the fish are going to bite and when the bait's gone. I'd be a millionaire."

By whatever means Iglesias strikes it rich, his goal is unchanged: to leave Venice Beach. The changes are becoming too much for him to stomach. Iglesias might have flipped to know that the Splatter Man shares some of the same sentiments for the trend the beach is taking.

"It's not always this nice around here. Like at night when the weird people come out, watch out," the Splatter Man said. ∎

26 CALIFORNIA

Saga of a Bit-Player

At first glance, the old guy looked like a typical vagrant milling inconspicuously among a crowd of gawkers watching a scene of *Magnum, P.I.* being filmed in a Venice Beach back alley. Most people strained to catch a glimpse of the show's star, Tom Selleck. But not the bum.

The bum appeared more interested in staring at pretty girls in the crowd than at Selleck. He had the layered look down pat: He wore a ratty brown coat with the sleeve linings torn and hanging out, over an outdated blue cardigan sweater, over a plaid sports shirt, over a blue cotton pullover. A felt hat sat atop his head. Strange garb for 85-degree weather.

That much you could deduce from a distance. But something about the old guy wasn't right. Up close, you noticed that he was clean-shaven, he didn't stink, and he had all his teeth. And the pocket of his ratty coat contained not a bottle, but an orange.

"You seen *Gone With The Wind*? I was in *Gone With The Wind*. Played a Union soldier in the burning of Atlanta, held up dummies of soldiers on each of my arms. Played a Confederate soldier in that one, too," said the bum, who is actually Mickey Golden, 77, Extra Actor Extraordinaire of West Hollywood.

Although he has 50 years of film experience, Golden finds that television is where he is most in demand — today *Magnum, P.I.*, tomorrow *Hill Street Blues*, next week *Cagney and Lacey*. When cast directors need a scruffy hobo in the background, an elderly passerby or a frightened man ducking bullets in a grocery store holdup, they call Golden.

He will earn $91 this day for standing around behind Selleck. On his assignment card is a single directive to the atmosphere (movie talk for extras such as Golden): "Do not approach Tom Selleck."

"They don't like actors like me bugging the big stars," Golden said, "but I know Selleck. He's a very nice man. He goes up to women all the time and kisses and hugs them."

Hmmm.

These days, Golden says, film work is catch-as-catch-can. But his memories of the Hollywood of years past, when movie moguls ran the business and

SOON A GUY WHO LOOKED A LITTLE BIT LIKE TOM SELLECK MADE HIS WAY THROUGH THE CROWD. IT WAS THE REAL TOM SELLECK, BUT HE DIDN'T LOOK AS MUCH LIKE HIMSELF AS HIS DOUBLE DID. HE SAID A FEW WORDS INTO A CLOSE-UP CAMERA (WHILE LEANING ON THE CAR) AND WAS ESCORTED QUICKLY AWAY WHILE THE CREW PACKED UP.

he was a busy actor at MGM, remain as vivid as yesterday's.

"It was a wonderful era when I came out here, the golden era of movie making," Golden said.

"Clark Gable, Robert Taylor, Greta Garbo, I'd see them all as they walked out of the MGM commissary. Gable was a nice man. Tony Quinn was great, too. Shoot, I was always going to Rory Calhoun's house in Beverly Hills for parties and dinner. Once I was with my wife, and she asked me, 'Do they know you're an extra?' I said, 'Sure, but they don't care. If they like you, then it doesn't matter if you're an extra or a star.'

"I'm a peasant at heart. I think that's what these guys liked about me," Golden said.

Born and reared in New York City, Golden went to California in 1934 with a group of fighters barnstorming the country. They called him the Irish Jew in appreciation of his sparing the face of an overmatched Irish boxer in a Knights of Columbus bout.

Golden said he just drifted into motion pictures, never making much money, but he managed to keep busy and live comfortably.

The Golden Era of Hollywood in the 1940s was among Golden's best years because it was then that he was befriended by actor/singer Mario Lanza. It was a friendship that lasted until Lanza's death in 1959.

Lanza was a big box office star in those years, and Golden's fortunes followed because he usually was Lanza's acting double onscreen. Offscreen, they often drove to locations together, and Lanza would sing opera for Golden's ears only.

Once Lanza, upon learning that Golden was earning only $17 a day, insisted that he buy Golden and his wife a new house. When Golden refused the offer, Lanza compromised by seeing to it that Golden received a parking lot pass at the MGM studio. It was among Golden's most cherished possessions.

"I guess you could say for a while I was a fair-haired boy at MGM during its heyday," Golden said. "I remember they'd come up to me with a script and say, 'Mr. Golden, here's your dialogue.' And I'd feel like a million bucks."

Golden has been an extra or a double in so many movies that he claims he has forgotten many of them.

"Name some movies, and I'll tell you whether I was in them," he urges.

Sure, he was in *The Sting*, hung up numbers on a horse racing betting board in the concluding scenes. He played George Segal's double in *King Rat*, an Egyptian in *Cleopatra*, a farmer in *Blazing Saddles*.

"I'll be sitting with my wife watching old pictures on TV at home, and she'll say, 'There you are.'

"Listen, I've had quite a few offers to write books. I don't think I'm interesting, but a lot of people do. Me, I just look at myself as a professional extra."

Now he's taking it easy, working only when he feels like it, spending most of his time puttering around his home or tooling around the neighborhood in his beat-up Dodge Colt.

"I could afford a Cadillac, but I like to stay low key, just kind of go along with life. At my age, you have to be that way." ■

WITH A BEACH TO GO TO EVERYDAY, THESE PEOPLE SHOULD BE A LOT FRIENDLIER THAN THE ONES I'VE MET.

HERE IN LOS ANGELES
THEY'VE GOT MORE
OCEAN THAN THEY CAN
POSSIBLY USE,
WHILE CINCINNATI AIN'T
GOT NO OCEAN AT ALL.

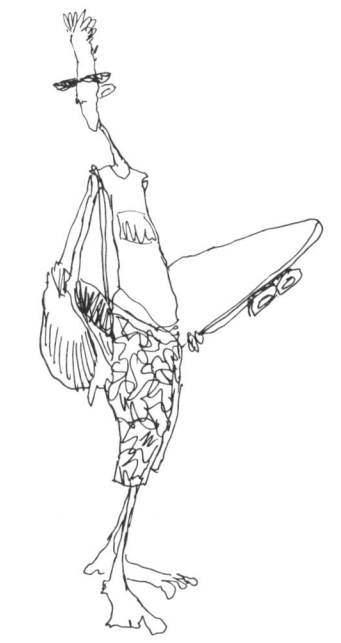

CALIFORNIA 31

Sun City, Arizona

It's 7 a.m. at the Marinette Recreation Center and the digital thermometer on the shaded wall reads 95.

People have been arriving for workouts since 4:30, but now is the busiest time of the day. Joggers and walkers dodge quail to trundle the cinder track solo or in pairs; women fill the pool looking like synchronized swimmers while performing their daily therapeutic regimen; and tennis players — faces flushed, shirts soaked — curse the shots their aging bodies no longer let them make.

In a couple of hours the temperature will be 100. By noon 110. The retirees of Sun City, like the coyotes, elf owls, sidewinders and other nocturnal creatures with whom they share their desert lives, have learned to adjust their schedules around the scorching heat.

At midday, the streets and recreation centers of this city of 40,000 near Phoenix will be as deserted as a ghost town. But now they are a whirlwind of activity.

"What was that?" calls out Jackie Dina, a former resident of Union Lakes, Mich., as her backhand shot sails well beyond the opposite base line. She has no backhand to speak of, and her seasoned opponents have been hitting to it all game.

"Long," comes the reply from across the net. Jackie stands staring into space as if she can't believe it.

Walking off an adjoining court, robust and ebullient after one set of doubles and ready for another, Jackie's husband, Richard, pooh-poohs his wife's misplays.

"I've been here 10 years, and I like it fine, except for all these damned old people. They drive you crazy. They walk in front of you, get in your way, fall under the wheels of your golf cart. It's terrible," said a straight-faced Richard Dina, a retired vice president at American Airlines who says he is "76, going on 17."

Dina speaks for all that is attractive and enjoyable about Sun City. He can poke fun at this huge retirement city built exclusively for senior citizens from nothing 26 years ago, and all those around him are going to laugh along with him.

Everyone who lives in the pleasant, pastel-shaded homes set along spotless streets lined with cactuses and palm trees is older than 50, but hardly squandering their twilight years. Sun City residents say they have to wait in line to attend church services, and the last election had a 76 percent voter turnout.

"We always like to see young people come around and visit . . . and then go home so we can get back to having fun," said Roy Smith, formerly of St. Edward, Neb. The Smiths and the Hitchcocks, formerly of Montrose, Pa., have just finished a match of lawn bowling under the lights at the Sundial Recreation Center. Lawn bowling, played on large plots of grass manicured as finely as golf putting greens, is a favorite

LAWN BOWLING
SUN CITY, ARIZONA

sport in Sun City after the sun goes down.

"Vacation every day, that's what it feels like," Smith said. "We don't even know when it's a holiday."

"I don't ever like to leave," said Irvin Hitchcock, a retired farmer who traded his tractor for a golf cart when he moved from Pennsylvania to Arizona. "When I do go home, I get homesick for Sun City and can't wait to get back."

For all its attractions, Sun City life revolves mainly around two subjects: health and heat.

"After you've been here a couple of months, you get used to the heat," said Dale Cody, who, as a native of Minnesota, speaks from experience.

"But we still look forward to going back home in July and August when it really gets hot here," he said.

"You couldn't end up in a nicer place in the whole U.S.," said Truman Herr, a native of Redwood City, Calif., who is stretching his legs in preparation for a round of tennis.

"It's just hot, that's all. But the humidity is so low. If you were out East in 95-degree weather, you'd be suffocating right about now. But look at me, I'm not even sweating," Herr said.

Other residents are not as enthralled with the change of scenery.

"I'm moving back to San Bernardino (Calif.) in a few months. It's too hot for me here," said Bill Jeffers, a retired businessman.

He walks briskly on the track with his wife, Dorothy, who laments that "everything drops dead at noon around here."

"Besides, no one told us before we moved here ▶

about the dust storms," Jeffers said. "They're bad for my respiratory condition. They laugh about them, call them 'Sun City monsoons.' But monsoons are supposed to have rain."

Jan Mittelstadt, editor of the *Daily News-Sun* in Sun City, said the Jeffers' reaction was common.

"Not everyone here has been as swept up with the way of life as they first thought they would be," Mittelstadt said. "Some people think it's depressing, just a lot of people waiting to die. But it's not that way at all."

Death, however, is a notable preoccupation among the residents. Dinners typically include discussions of wills and who is suffering from what in which Sun City hospital.

The Sun City business districts are distinct, too, reflecting the needs of its residents. The city has an abundance of banks, investment agencies, hospitals, doctors offices and eye clinics and at least six handicapped parking spots per retail establishment. Notably absent are theaters, video arcades and fast-food restaurants.

Without the advent of air-conditioning it's likely that the primary occupants of this desert community and much of the Southwest would still be lizards, tumbleweeds, gunfighters and cattle rustlers. As late as 1940, Phoenix was a minor outpost of 65,000. By 1980, it had become a metro area of 1.5 million and the ninth-largest city in the nation.

Growth in the area brought typical big city problems to Sun City: litter and crime. Sun City residents responded to these blights with two of the most popular volunteer activities, the Sun City Prides and the Sheriff's Posse. The Prides scour the city picking up litter, lending credence to its claim as the cleanest city in the nation; the posse comprises 240 elderly deputies who patrol the city.

Posse Commander Bert Brosius says the city's 3.2 percent crime rate makes it the safest in the nation.

"Some people think that after 50, you're a has-been. We're proving them wrong," said Brosius, a retired communications executive for the Bell System in Washington, D.C. ▶

ARIZONA 35

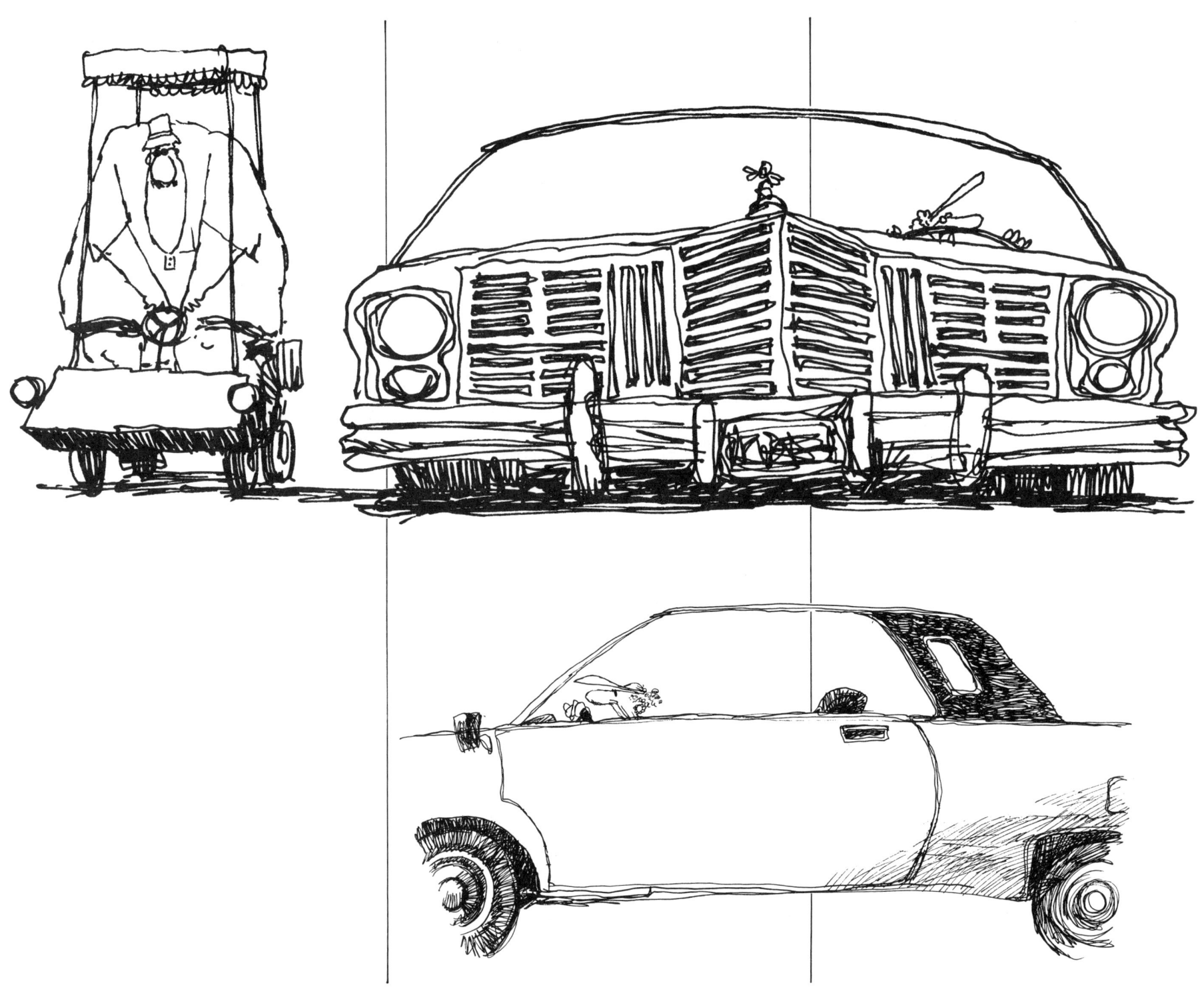

"Every now and then we'll catch a cat burglar," he said. "And we are constantly fighting the door-to-door scam artists who try to take advantage of the elderly. When we catch them, we run them out of town and follow them to make sure they leave.

"Our own people in Sun City are pretty good. It's the people who live outside the city and come in who we have to worry about."

Although gray, the deputies command respect. Dutch Schultz, a retired country singer who volunteers as a deputy, wrote the posse theme song that boasts:

We may be gray, but we still got the stuff
To do a job when the going is rough.
It's a lot of work and not much fun
But the pleasure we get is a job well done.

Many posse deputies are retired lawyers, accountants and office workers; about 45 are female. Included on the roster of citizens who volunteer as deputies for the posse is one President Ronald Reagan. Few deputies are former lawmen, and Brosius prefers it that way. Otherwise, he figures he would have to spend a lot of time breaking them of old techniques and teaching them the way things are done in Sun City.

"We have one of the best shooting ranges in the valley, and I would put our people up against anyone," Brosius said.

Posse deputies are called on by the Maricopa County sheriff to help break up big parties in the desert, set up DWI roadblocks, shake down prostitutes and transport prisoners. More often, deputies are called on to search for lost and disoriented elderly people. Because a third of Sun City's residents escape to cooler climates during the summer, the deputies frequently check houses, he said.

For those residents who prefer not to mix it up with criminals or pick up trash, there are lots of other enjoyable recreation activities, such as arts and crafts, cards, dancing, music, service and social groups.

For the sports-minded there are golf — both mini and standard — indoor and outdoor bowling, bocce, billiards, handball and racquetball, horseshoes, swimming, shuffleboard, jogging and tennis, both table and court. Most are enjoyed in the cool of early morning or evening darkness.

Sunset begins the favorite time of the day for Warren Samet, formerly of Long Island, N.Y., who with his wife and friends, relishes kicking up his heels, blowing on his clarinet and belting out a rendition of tunes at a variety of dances and big band concerts held several nights a week in Sun City.

"Rock-a-bye your baby with a Dixie melody," Samet sings as if on cue for all within earshot of the Marinette Recreation Center.

Samet ignores Richard Dina, who chides him with "he just likes to throw a lot of hot air around."

"Music is our life," Samet says. "That's why we came here." ■

SWIMMING AT THE REC CENTER — SUN CITY, ARIZONA

ARIZONA 37

Fear and Slithering in the Arizona Desert

by Jim Borgman

An hour's drive north out of Phoenix lands you in the mutant beauty of the dusty, desolate Southwestern desertlands. There, Tonto National Forest stands as a monument to every black-and-white cowboy movie ever shown on Saturday afternoon television. The ground sizzles. If you were going to pick a mountain to blow up you would likely guess one of these flame-broiled beasts, simmering in this barking 110° heat.

On the day we drove out there the sun was so intense that I kept checking in the rearview mirror to make sure it was my sunglasses I was wearing.

We stopped first at the ranger station in Carefree, Arizona (famous, of course, for the sugarless gum that runs from the local cacti).

"The wildlife's pretty hard to find during the day," the ranger told us. "You'll see some quail, maybe a roadrunner or elf owl," she said. The sun is too hot for much activity. But the critters are out there. One ranger had seen a bobcat the day before. There are coyotes and hawks, too.

"And lots of snakes."

Lots of snakes. The only concept more frightening to me than snakes is lots of snakes. A desertful of snakes under rocks is beyond the limits of my adrenalin. I imagined them leaping off of cacti onto me, springing from holes in the dry ground.

My fellow traveller, Jim McCarty, is a birdwatcher. His eyes and ears roam skyward when not preoccupied at ground level. As we drove the miles of dirt roads into the heart of snakeland he looked for gray cardinals and scrub jays. My eyes were aimed at those flat rocks. Most of them were moving. What if I ran over a snake and it got wrapped around in the axle and the car wouldn't move?

The first sign of malevolence was an old horny toad who darted from behind a saguaro cactus (saguaro is an Indian word meaning, 'run like hell, there are snakes all around you') and barely out of the path of our car. McCarty picked the monster up on his road atlas. Its mouth stood open in reptilian disgust.

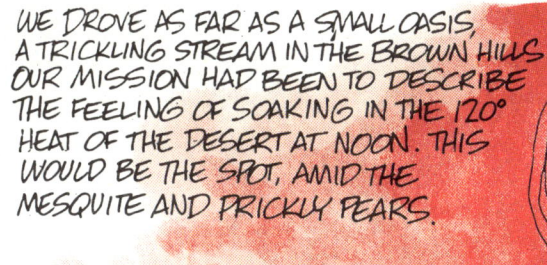

We drove as far as a small oasis, a trickling stream in the brown hills. Our mission had been to describe the feeling of soaking in the 120° heat of the desert at noon. This would be the spot, amid the mesquite and prickly pears.

The heat penetrated, seared the hairs on our arms. The wire rims of my glasses burned my temples. I wanted to carry home a colorful stone, but I couldn't hold it. I looked up through a juniper tree at the fierce sky and I saw a snake. In a tree. Above my head.

I have to assume this was one of a variety of poisonous, flesh-eating, fast-moving snakes that coils around its prey, slowly squeezing the life out of its grossed-out victim. I have to assume this because it was in a tree above my head.

Catclaw mimosas scratched my wheeling legs. If this snake had my number it was probably alerting all the others nearby. Snakes can smell fear, you know, but not through the windows of a Ford Tempo.

So what was the feeling of soaking in the 120° heat of the desert at noon from inside a car parked in the sun with the windows rolled up?

Just delightful, thank you.

Fort Worth, Texas

Because they're so close together, it's easy for non-Texans to lump Fort Worth with Dallas, its larger, more cosmopolitan partner in eastern Texas. But Texans know that residents of the two cities, 28 miles apart, mix about as well as oil and water.

People from Dallas consider themselves more sophisticated than their Fort Worth neighbors, whom they tend to classify as cowboys in a cow town. Most Fort Worth residents won't argue with that label, either.

"Fort Worth is where the West begins; Dallas is where the East peters out," drawls Terry Arnold between swigs from a bottle of Dr Pepper.

To illustrate the clear superiority of his hometown, Arnold tells the story of Jerry Pippen, a friend who was attacked by a wild boar while hunting quail in western Texas. Ol' Jerry scaled a small tree to save his skin, all the while kicking the boar.

But the vicious boar clamped its sharp fangs into Jerry's boot and refused to release its vise-grip. A hunting companion put an end to the adventure with a single shot to the boar's heart.

"Today," said Arnold, practically bursting with glee, "Jerry has that mama boar's head mounted on his wall with his boot still stuck in its mouth. I ask you, would an oil slicker from Dallas do that?"

"Terry, you're wittier than I thought you were. You're pretty good," says Ludy Bush, a cashier at Pete Riscky's Barbeque, where the tasty ribs are legend in the historic but declining area around Fort Worth's stockyards.

Bush likes trading yarns with Arnold, a bearded real estate salesman in his late 30s who wears a cheap straw hat and a $600 pair of ostrich skin boots. Arnold has been a fixture at the barbeque ever since Pete Riscky gave him his first job as a youngster stacking soda bottles. Arnold has been passing a lot more of his time here in recent months since the home-buying market slumped, but he remains unfazed.

"Everyone goes down sooner or later, but Texas always bounces back up," Arnold said confidently.

When he steps away, Bush whispers that Arnold

UNBROKEN HORSE

was once married to Diane Wills, daughter of Bob Wills, the king of Texas Swing and a country music legend. Wills even lived with the Arnolds for four years, and country singers Ernest Tubb and Merle Haggard were frequent house guests.

There was a time, too, when Willie Nelson lived in the same Fort Worth neighborhood, Bush says. She recalls how Nelson used to supplement his then-meager singing income by selling encyclopedias to residents along nearby Jacksboro Highway.

Those were better days for Fort Worth. Trains left the stockyards every day pulling long lines of cars packed with livestock bound for slaughterhouses in Denver, Tulsa and Chicago. The stockyards stretched for a mile, all the way from the tracks to the highway, packed with cattle, hogs, sheep and horses. A good gauge of success was in the air all around — the unmistakable, nose-tingling pungent odor of fresh manure.

"Until I went into the Navy in San Diego in '67, I thought all the air was supposed to smell like that," Arnold said.

A stockyards visitor almost has to step in a pile of manure to smell it today. Once the nation's leading center of livestock trade, tracing all the way back to the days of the Chisholm Trail in the Old West, the city's stockyards now take up a fraction of their former space and do but a small percentage of their previous business.

But elements of the area's storybook past remain strong and true. Drive 20 miles in any direction seven nights a week and you'll still find a rodeo. There's even a wanted poster on a stockyards office wall advertising a search for a scruffy-looking cattle rustler named Perry Alvin Alexander.

"You can tell he got away with it — he's smilin'," said Steve Cook, only glancing at the faded poster while seeking a brief respite from the heat and humidity outside.

Cook is a wrangler, an old-fashioned bronco-busting cowboy in every sense of the word. He started riding milk calves with the Breckenridge Little Britches at age 6, worked his way up through the big-time rodeo circuit after high school and stuck with it, touring the country and performing as a professional until 1983.

"I finally got a little sense knocked into me. It started to hurt so much, I had to get out of it," Cook said.

Now 27 and retired from the rodeo, Cook has been breaking horses for auction at the stockyards for the last six months.

"It's a good life," said Cook, clearly experienced at speaking with a load of snuff packed inside his lower lip. "Where else are you going to find the kind of freedom I have? And horses don't talk back to you. They'll kick you, buck you and spit on you, but they don't talk back."

By noon, Cook has worked out three horses. He has two wild ones still left for the afternoon. Those that learn to follow directions and accept a rider will bring about $4,500 at auction. Those that don't will be sold for $300 and end up in a can of dog food.

Cook despises new and violent horse training techniques such as shocking horses with cattle prods, hitting them between the ears with a stick or tying them to another horse, all of which can injure the ▶

TEXAS 41

STORYTELLER
TERRY ARNOLD
AT PETE RISCKY'S
BAR-B-Q

LUDY BUSH
RISCKY'S CHECKOUT CLERK

BILLY WHITE
IN THE FORT WORTH
STOCKYARD OFFICE

animal. He prefers the traditional ways but draws the line at pampering a horse.

Cook tells of a 2-year-old horse he agreed to train for a woman who had "spoiled it rotten," raising the horse to think it was a human. Every morning, the horse would stick its head out a window, and the woman would kiss it on the nose, he said.

"I told the lady that I'd do all she wanted as far as training that horse went, but there wasn't any amount of money she could pay to convince me to kiss that horse on the nose every morning," Cook said.

Cook demonstrates his training technique for us, emphasizing the need for patience. He stalks a frisky golden-tan mare around a dusty ring, taking his time, clicking his tongue, reassuring her, letting her jump around at will to tire her out.

"You've got to do everything real slow. If you move

WRANGLER
STEVE COOK
FORT WORTH STOCKYARDS

OLD GOAT IN PICKUP TRUCK
FORT WORTH, TEXAS

fast, she's going to jump," he says.

Finally, the mare lets him approach. He pats her flanks and ever so slowly mounts the saddle. The horse snorts and bucks and paws the earth, but she doesn't throw Cook, and soon he is guiding her around the corral by her reins.

"These are the kind of horses I like — whoa, don't buck — whoa." He spoke too soon.

In the stockyards office — a brick shack, really, with a corrugated tin roof and an air-conditioner that blows lukewarm air on an array of worn, stuffed chairs covered with cigarette burns — Billy White says he thinks he knows where the stockyards are headed.

"This will all be gone before you know it. We keep getting smaller, and every town around has a livestock auction now and keeps getting bigger," said White, a stockyards hand in his 50s who has worked here since high school. "On the weekends it's such a hassle, traders who come here have to wade through parking lots filled with tourists' cars. It's much easier to go to Bowie or one of the other auctions."

All the stockyards hands point accusing fingers at Billy Bob's, a sprawling converted slaughterhouse that is billed as the world's largest honky-tonk bar. It features 42 separate bar stations, seating for 6,000, ▶

Steve Cook slowly mounts an unbroken horse in the red brick stable of the Fort Worth Stockyards

44 TEXAS

rooms full of arcade games and a live indoor rodeo that converts to a church service on Sundays.

Tourists by the thousands park their cars in the stockyards' lots next door. White and Cook complain that the tourists often open the pens and let the livestock escape. The two realize, however, that without the tourists coming to Billy Bob's, there might be nothing left of the stockyards area.

Others have a more positive outlook. Bob Chandler, a 72-year-old sheep rancher who has been coming to the Fort Worth stockyards for almost 50 years, said, "This year has been about as good a year for sheep as I've seen in a long time."

Chandler is not nostalgic for years gone by, because in most of them, he says, livestock ranchers failed to make a profit.

"They may be the good old days for some people, but I had to work too hard back then to make a living. If those were the good old days, they can have them," Chandler said.

Although people like Chandler weren't eager to revive the good ol' days, nearly everyone around Fort Worth was eagerly waiting to celebrate them on the Fourth of July. A huge jubilee was planned, capped by the arrival at the stockyards of 150 Conestoga wagons scheduled to complete a six-month journey around the state. The trip was in honor of Texas' sesquicentennial.

Of course, some like Cook claim to have a streak of renegade left in them.

"I'd rather be at the Statue of Liberty this Fourth. It would be nice for a change. This gets old after awhile.

"But I'm sure I'll have a good time here, too," he said. "The way people are around here, if somebody finds out about your birthday you're going to have a party whether you want to or not. And when you're single, all the married women try to get you married off, so you're never lacking for entertainment.

"Sure, times are tough for everyone, but we all stick together around these parts." ■

BILLY WHITE WITH YOUNG CATTLE

SOLD YESTERDAY AT AUCTION TO A FEED LOT, THESE CATTLE WILL GAIN 250 POUNDS IN THE NEXT MONTH.

TEXAS 45

46 TEXAS

Stalking the Wild Armadillo
by Jim Borgman

Pasty-brown carcasses of armadillos gone to their reward dot the roadsides of Texas like possums or squirrels in the Midwest. Comparatively, the armadillos remain cute, their hard bodies intact, posing with arms, legs and tails askew.

After what I saw last night, their roadside fate seems only fair.

Etta Hulme, cartoonist at the *Fort Worth Star-Telegram*, briefed me on getting a closer look. Armadillos have few things going for them. They have poor sight and bad hearing and walk slowly and awkwardly. Their sense of smell is good, but from downwind, you could walk right up and put a box over them. Their only defense is rolling up in a ball and hoping danger goes away. Many wear pacemakers, too, and suffer from itchy, flaking dandruff. Most stutter.

No sweat.

It was dusk when McCarty and I drove into the wet, wooded land on the edge of Lake Worth. Fog lay in the low spots on the road, and wild dogs howled in the distance. A queer sense of doom hung in the air, confusing our whimsical mission to stalk the wild armadillo.

As we walked the deserted road away from our rented car, the flashlight fell upon an old shoe, not unlike the ones on my own feet. This one was ripped to shreds and lay in a puddle of murky water. A little further on a red gym sock lay across the yellow line.

"They've been here, alright," McCarty said, "and they take no prisoners."

One hundred feet down the road we spotted the other shoe near a narrow path into the woods.

"Gawd," I thought, "they dragged the poor devil."

We must have stood dead still for an hour, listening only to the beating of our hearts and the chatter of what we took to be armadillo laughter.

When we moved again, it was only a moment before we saw our first armadillo. From the way he lumbered across the road, I expected to see him dragging on a cigarette and carrying a lunch pail. He seemed not to see us, and we followed him into a dense woods where he disappeared.

All that we found was a smoldering campfire, half a bottle of tequila and a freshly dealt hand of five-card stud. Little tiny cards. And a pack of Tiparillos. Armadillo Tiparillos.

It was hours later in the thick of a Texas night that we heard rustling in the woods all around us. The leaves shook. Something heavy splashed in the lake behind us. A minute later we realized the camera was gone.

We had lost their track completely. Worse, the little demons were messing with our minds.

When we found the car in the swampy darkness down the embankment, it was upside down. Shredded rubber hung where the tires had been. No sign remained of an interior. The chrome was stripped.

A scribbled note was slammed in the door. This is what it said:

G-G-G-GET OUT!

EVOLUTION HAS PLAYED A DIRTY TRICK ON ARMADILLOS. WHEN ALARMED, THEIR INSTINCT IS TO JUMP STRAIGHT UP INTO THE AIR......

......ABOUT GRILL-LEVEL ON THESE BIG TEXAS CARS.

Armadillo Sketchbook
by Jim Borgman

TEXAS ROADSIDE SKETCHBOOK

48 TEXAS

MORE TEXAS ROADSIDE

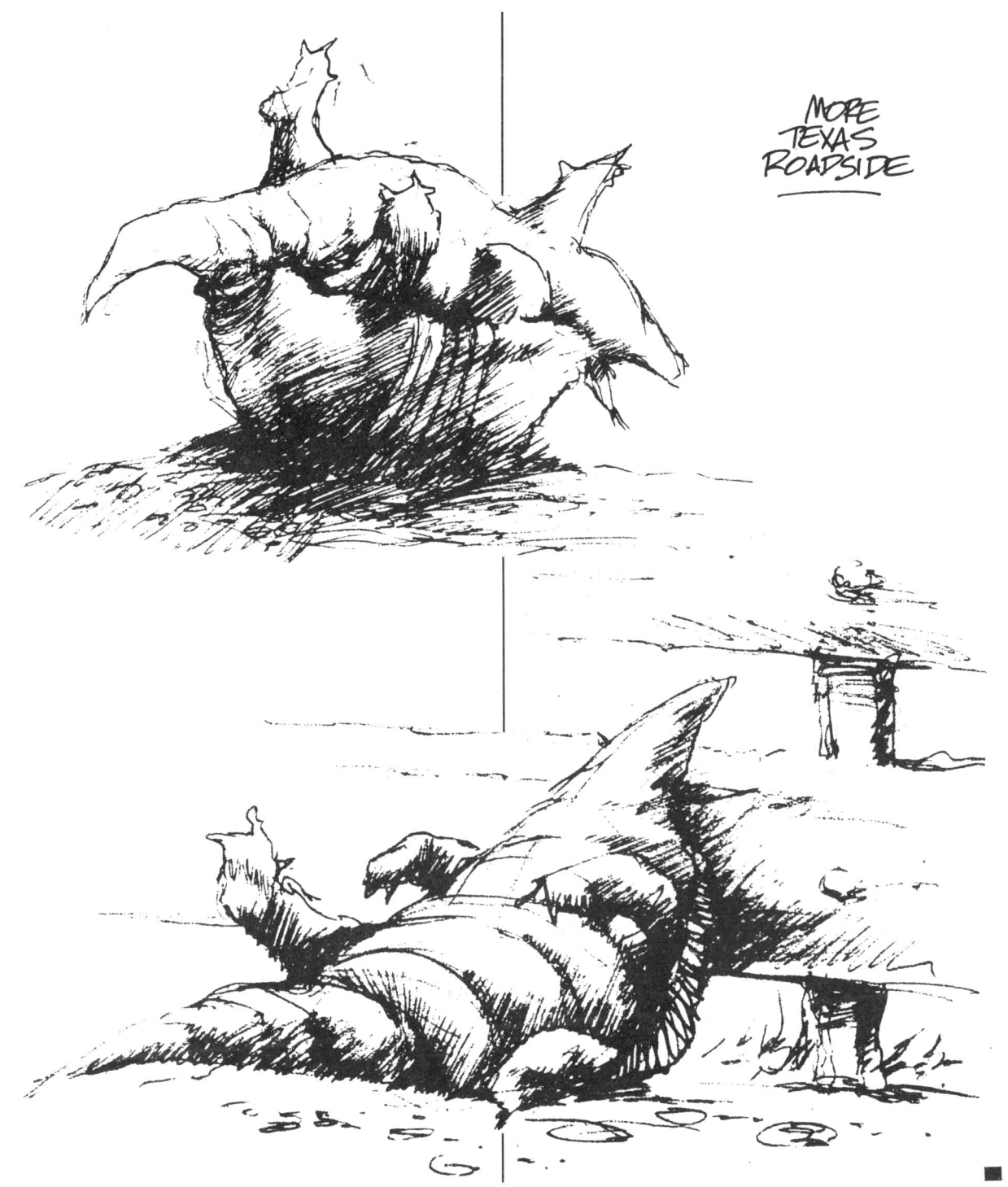

TEXAS 49

Denver, Colorado

SECURITY GUARD
DENVER ZEPHYRS NIGHT GAME

A Night in the Minors

Life on the farm can be wonderful. Baseball remains more a game than a business at the foot of the Rocky Mountains, where the Denver Zephyrs — the Reds' AAA farm team — play a zany brand of baseball.

Fans of the Z's, as they are known here, have come to expect a bit of the offbeat with their peanuts and hot dogs. Three of the all-time clown princes of the game, Casey Stengel, Billy Martin and Marvelous Marv Throneberry, are Denver veterans.

Whether it's the thin air, some mysterious mountain magnetism or all that Coors beer in the clubhouse cooler, the national pastime takes on a unique flavor in this football-crazy town.

On this day, Bob Howsam Jr., the Zephyrs' president and general manager, is brainstorming with Greg Corns, his right-hand man. Here's Howsam's predicament:

If magical forces won't come to bat for his team at tonight's game, shouldn't he dream up a scheme of his own to tip the odds in the Zephyrs' favor?

Howsam snickers. He already has a plan. He'll arm his players with squirt guns and order them to shoot the opposing pitcher. Howsam knows that it's smart baseball to stick with what works, and he can hardly count on a stroke of good fortune such as occurred the night before.

The game had started out badly, with the first place Z's falling behind the Omaha Royals, Kansas City's farm team, by two runs in the fourth inning. Opposing ▶

50 COLORADO

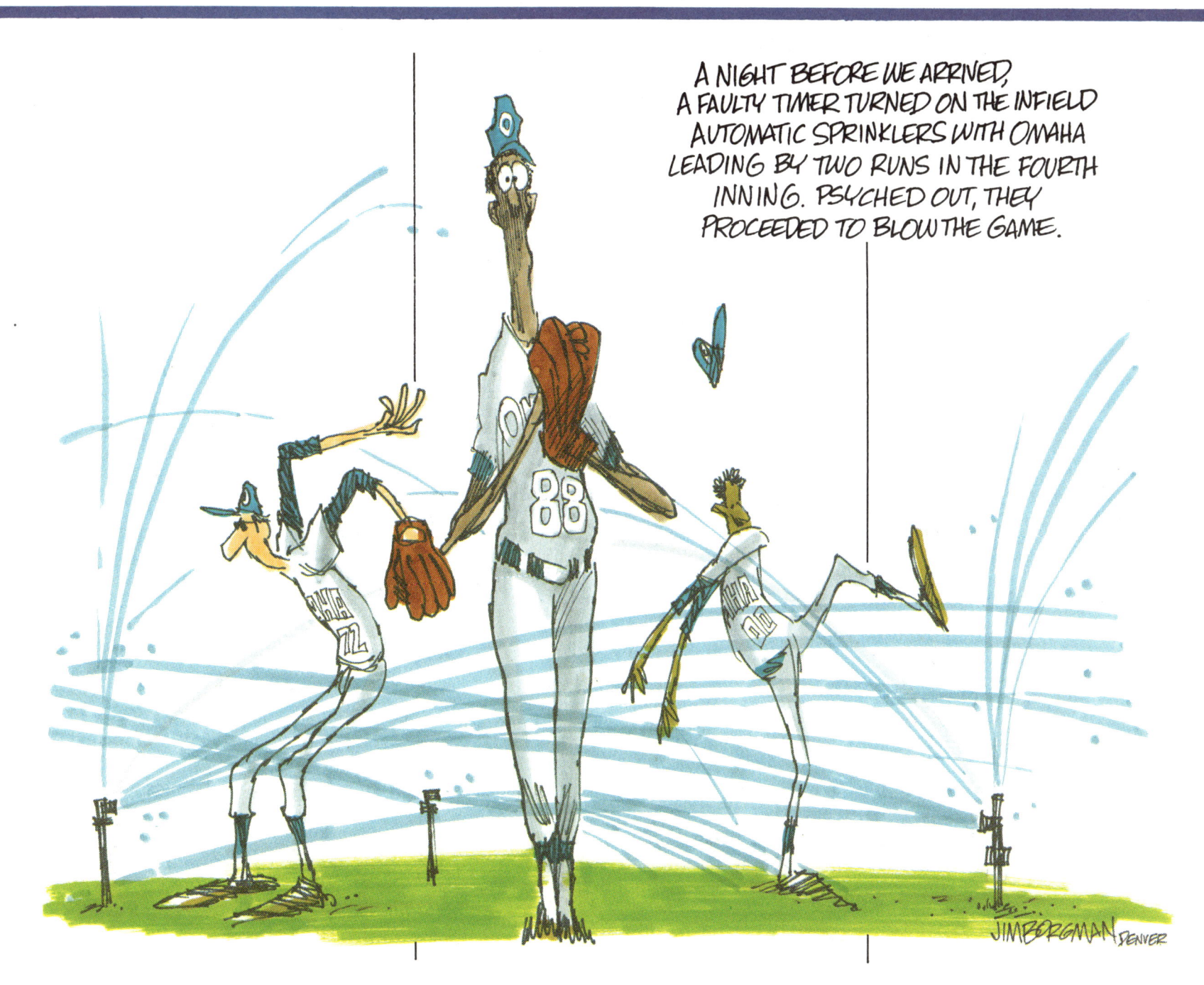

A night before we arrived, a faulty timer turned on the infield automatic sprinklers with Omaha leading by two runs in the fourth inning. Psyched out, they proceeded to blow the game.

HUNDREDS OF HANDICAPPED KIDS WERE GUESTS OF THE ZEPHYRS AT THE BALLPARK, AND PLAYERS SPENT THE HOUR BEFORE GAMETIME ROLLING THEM GROUNDBALLS IN THE OUTFIELD GRASS AND TEACHING THEM ABOUT FIELDING. THE KIDS SHOUTED THE NAMES OF THEIR BASEBALL HEROES AS THEY FIELDED THE BALLS:

"ROWDON!"
"MCGRIFF!"
"STEVE GARVEY!"
"VAN GORDER!"

AT FIVE MINUTES TILL GAME TIME, PLAYERS WERE STILL SIGNING AUTOGRAPHS IN A SEA OF HAPPY KIDS.

pitcher Keefe Cato was in a groove, mowing down the home team's batters.

Then, for no apparent reason, the field's sprinkler system jumped to life, swishing and squirting long shots of water around the infield, dousing the pitcher and his teammates.

All were stunned. Pandemonium broke out, and cavernous Mile High Stadium echoed with laughter.

Howsam was furious. "I got on the phone to our groundskeeper and I yelled, 'What the hell is going on out there?'"

It turned out to be a timer malfunction.

The brief episode had a surprising result. The sprinkler cooled off the opposing pitcher; he grew flustered, and the Z's batters started to powder his pitches. The Z's won the game, 9-5.

Howsam hoped his players could recreate the previous night's events with squirt guns. A more serious approach to the game prevailed, however.

"OK men, put your guns back in your holsters," ordered manager Jack Lind, calling the team together for a pregame meeting.

For the previous half hour, the Zephyrs' locker room under the right-field bleachers had been a battle zone. Some of the young players were shooting their new toys at anyone who moved.

As it turned out, the pregame dousing cooled off the wrong team. The Z's lost, 6-5, to the high and dry second-place Royals, cutting their lead to one game.

No need to worry. It's only one game. We'll get 'em tomorrow. Just be sure everyone has a good time . . . and don't forget your squirt guns.

"This is what makes minor league baseball fun," said Howsam, a natty dresser in silk tie and suspenders. "We're open for anything. We'll do anything it takes to bring people in, but we prefer to do it with a little bit of class."

That's a difficult task. On the field, with few exceptions, the team members would rather be playing in Riverfront Stadium. In the stands, most fans, given a preference, would rather be watching the Broncos play football, the Nuggets play basketball or their own major league team play baseball, in that order.

The Z's average about 3,000 fans in a stadium that seats 70,000. A foul ball to the upper deck easily can go unclaimed for an inning while a youngster scales the steps and tracks the ball down amid empty seats.

One reader explained his theory on the Zephyrs' attendance problems in a letter to the *Denver Post*: "I find it hard to cheer for a team called the Zephyrs with a straight face. I don't know if this is the same reason others don't go, but I know it's mine."

A zephyr, by the way, is a west wind.

"I'm real frustrated we can't seem to land a major league franchise," said Jerry Stratton, a loyal Z's fan from nearby Littleton, Colo., who is seated behind home plate. "I think this would be an ideal major league park. Sure, there would be lots of home runs hit in the thin air but that would be all right." ▶

A SINGLE VENDOR SELLS HOT DOGS, PEANUTS AND BEER. SURE ENOUGH, HE HAD THE CATSUP AND MUSTARD TOO.

A SIX-YEAR-OLD BOY SAT ON THE ZEPHYRS DUGOUT AND NO ONE TOLD HIM TO MOVE.

Stratton, 50, a high school English teacher, spends his summers as an umpire at softball games and a spectator at Zephyrs' and sandlot games. In short, he's a baseball fanatic.

"Anybody who says baseball's not the national pastime doesn't know the statistics. It's my favorite sport.

"I still get goose bumps at old-timers' games. And even after all these years, I can get very sentimental, all misty eyed at a game, like when George Brett hits a homer," Stratton said.

Stratton has a definite distaste for domed stadiums and artificial surfaces. The Zephyrs' field is natural grass and immaculate, although the stadium itself was clearly built for football.

"I don't like that AstroTurf a bit; it's too synthetic, too new-tech," he said. "And I don't like those enclosed parks either. I like seeing the sky and the buildings and the mountains in the distance. Give me that much, and a beer, and I'm happy."

Stratton displays his knowledge of Denver weather when, just as he predicted it would, the dark storm clouds that have been hanging over the stadium for much of the afternoon clear up by game time, 7:05. The crowd, as usual, is small but vocal.

"I wish more people came to the games," admits shortstop Barry Larkin, seated at his locker before the game.

Larkin, a graduate of Cincinnati's Moeller High School, is regarded as a jewel in the Reds' farm system, and it's easy for even a casual fan to see why. He plays the game with an intense, often fierce, demeanor, spiking the ball a la Pete Rose after running down a base runner on one play, later thrusting a fist into the air after knocking a two-run double off the top of the 375 sign in left-center.

"I feel like I've gained a lot of confidence in my game and that's why I'm doing well," he said. He was batting .309 at the time. "It's been fun, but I'd rather be playing in Cincinnati. I'd like to get there tomorrow, get loose and see how it is so when I'm up there for good I won't be overwhelmed.

"I'm having fun; that's the most important thing."

One player who wasn't having much fun on the farm was former Reds catcher Dave Van Gorder. He was sent down to mend a broken wrist.

"At this point I really don't know what to think. I ▶

OMAHA OUTFIELDER MIKE KINGERY HIT A THREE-RUN HOMER (APPROPRIATELY) THROUGH THE UPRIGHTS OF THE DENVER BRONCOS' GOAL POST IN RIGHTFIELD.

FAMILY OF SEVEN ON THE BENCHES AT THE ZEPHYRS GAME.

ON THE DAY OF THE GAME WE PICKED UP SEATS IN ROW 2 BEHIND THE ZEPHYR DUGOUT FOR $5 EACH. THE BENCHES ARE CHEAPER STILL.

56 COLORADO

never used to like coming in here before, and I can't say I feel any different now," said Van Gorder, who at 29 is the senior member of the Z's.

"But I have to say, of all the minor league teams I've ever been with, this has to be one of the most relaxed," he said.

No sooner does Van Gorder say that than a squirt of water hits him in the face.

"I think some of the younger players look to me for advice, but I prefer to go to them and try to help them through some of the things I learned. Obviously they know how to play ball to get here. They just need a little extra mental push," he said.

On the mound tonight for the Z's is Pat Pacillo, a friendly former Olympian and No. 1 draft choice from North Jersey. As the game's starter he gets to choose the pregame music — his is Springsteen, of course.

The second Royals batter of the game knocks Pacillo's pitch for a home run to left. He serves up two more home runs before a trip to the showers in the fifth, down 5-0. The Z's lose, 6-5.

"The competition is much better up here than in (Double A) Vermont," Pacillo said before the game. "A lot of players have been there (in the majors), and a lot are on the verge of being there.

"I'm sure everybody thinks about going up to the Reds, but you've got to take care of business out here first. You've got to be patient. We're here for a reason."

Finally, there is pitcher Rob Murphy, a part-time Red, who for the second consecutive year has had his photograph dropped by mistake from the Zephyrs' game program. This year, the wide, smiling face of infielder Ron Henika has accidentally been put in Murphy's place.

"Two years in a row," Murphy shakes his head in mock disgust. "My mom's not pleased at all. And when she realizes Henika's head is so big . . . I mean he answers to the nickname Fred Flintstone . . . well, I'm afraid to think what she might do."

Mrs. Murphy could urge her son to take his squirt gun and shoot Howsam or whoever was responsible for the mistake in the program. Almost anything goes in the frolicking life on the farm. ■

NOBODY EVER DID ASK FOR OUR TICKETS.

COLORADO 57

Dixon, Illinois

The older women volunteers who lead tours of President Reagan's boyhood home on South Hennepin Avenue tried to steer us away from Johnny Humphreys.

"You don't want to talk to him" was the only explanation Lillian Peterson offered about the old man who runs an antique store on Galena Avenue, a couple of blocks away.

A few minutes with the outspoken Humphreys revealed what the women didn't want us to hear.

Humphreys is a Chamber of Commerce's nightmare, a free-talker who likes to reminisce about how Reagan's shoe salesman father was a heavy drinker who rarely paid the rent and how everyone knew that "Dutch" Reagan was a good-hearted boy, if not especially bright.

Humphreys says he speaks for many of Dixon's residents whose high expectations when Reagan was elected in 1980 have declined into despair. They resent the president for turning his back on his own, Humphreys said.

The quality of life for the people of this down-and-out Midwestern farming and factory city of 15,000 was headed downhill before Reagan was elected, and nothing he has done since then has altered that spiral, Humphreys said.

"They still respect Ronald Reagan, but they thought when he went to Washington that he'd remember his boyhood home. They thought we'd get all kinds of government grants and improved policies going for us. I knew that wouldn't be right to expect, but these people can be ignorant," said Humphreys, 77. He sits behind a cluttered antique desk with his feet propped up, fiddling with a thick silver and ruby medallion around his neck, spicing his speech with profanity.

Humphreys ticked off a roll call of Dixon's dead and dying: A wire mill has closed, a cement plant keeps changing hands and a milk plant has been sold in recent years. A shoe manufacturing plant is on its last legs, and the plight of the farmer is as bad here as anywhere.

"Without the farmer, this town is dead, and that's why we're hurting so bad," Humphreys said.

Reagan is aware of Dixon's problems because, Humphreys says, he keeps him informed.

"See this here?" He points to a hand-scribbled note on his cash register. "That's Ron's private number at the White House. Every week I call him 'cause he likes to keep in touch with what's happening back here."

"I usually do most of the talking. He doesn't tell me anything 'cause he knows I'm smarter than he is," Humphreys says with confidence. "Ron is a good guy, but the reason he's a good president is because he has good advisers around him."

Around the block from Humphrey's antique store Robert Hada, a newcomer from Rockford, operates a diner. Hada found that although many local people idolize Reagan, others are bitter. The walls of his restaurant and other downtown establishments are noticeably devoid of photographs of Reagan.

"You see a lot of people hurting bad around here. I think he could do much more for all the people who are out of work in Dixon," Hada said. "Reagan sure helped put Dixon on the map. I just wish people could have capitalized on it a little more.

"This is a good town, you couldn't find a friendlier place. They took us in like we were brothers and sisters. But to me, it looks like a dying town."

As a youth, "Dutch" Reagan was popular around town. He was a caddy at the country club and later a lifeguard, a regular attendant of First Christian Church and a talented athlete. As a hobby, he raised pigeons and rabbits with his older brother, "Moon."

"I knew him, but he didn't know me," said Peterson, who admitted having a schoolgirl crush on the tall, slim Reagan. "Oh, he was a handsome kid, but not what you would call a macho man. In fact, I think his girlfriend at the time was the preacher's daughter."

Peterson said she often would parade with her girlfriends back and forth under the lifeguard stand while Reagan watched over the swimmers at Lowell Park on the Rock River. Reagan saved 77 people from the river's swift currents during his lifeguard career, she said. Today the river is too polluted for swimming.

"He was never a rascal like some of the other boys; everyone trusted him, and I think he enjoyed the responsibility. I see some of those same qualities in him today. I really think he enjoys this president job," she said.

Everyone here agrees that despite the problems in Dixon, Reagan remains an extremely popular president.

"He's able to stay real popular in spite of everything because he's a wonderful politician. Like Roosevelt and Kennedy, you've got to have a knack and a know-how to put it over, like with the blasting of the Arabs," Humphreys said, pronouncing Arabs with a hard "A" and the accent on the first syllable. "He put it over, and he quieted them down. Hell, I think he ought to hit them again."

Reagan's popularity is reflected by the interest in his boyhood home. Since it opened two years ago, 60,000 people have visited the comfortable, two-story white house where Reagan lived.

Outside the house, Larry and Joyce Cravens of Media, Ill., waited to become the 68th and 69th people of the day to take the tour.

"When Reagan came into control, America was feeling pretty low, and he snapped us out of it pretty fast," said Cravens, a retired Marine. "He just simply says what people want to hear. He's a hard-core old Midwesterner and very genuine."

"He is the Great Communicator with those old-fashioned values," said Mrs. Craven, who twice voted against Reagan and doesn't regret either vote. She said she has two sons serving in the U.S. Army, and she fears for their safety.

"I just want him to be careful with my boys," she said.

The Cravens said they planned to leave Dixon after the tour, following the advice of Peterson to avoid Humphreys' antique store/souvenir shop. Had they chosen to shop there they could have purchased official Ronald Reagan inauguration medals or post cards, pictures, paintings or posters, buttons, plaques, plates, ash trays, pen holders, thermometers, spoons, bells, salt and pepper shakers, mugs, book bags, pocket knives, thimbles or, last but not least, official Ronald Reagan pot holders.

"In a few years, this stuff will be collectors' items," Humphreys says. ■

Halfway

We could hardly believe our ears. "That will be $63.58, sir. Cash or charge?"

The previous few hours in the Memphis Sheraton hadn't been a joy — just another edition of Borgman and McCarty on exhibit. Check-out time was noon; our dirty laundry wouldn't be clean until 4; our flight to St. Louis was at 6; and we still had lots of work to do. So we worked in the hotel lobby; he drawing, I typing, all the while a steady flow of people with time to spare watching the show.

We ignored our audience; it was worth the hassle — anything for clean clothes. It had been more than a week since we last tossed our dirty shirts, pants, underwear and socks into a coin-operated washing machine in Santa Monica, Calif. This time we opted for the hotel's valet service, which sent our clothing out.

Now our laundry was done, and the hotel clerk wanted $63.58 for the service. We were speechless.

"We could have bought a new wardrobe for that price," we protested. But faced with the prospect of another day without clean clothes, we gave in, charging it to the company credit card, naturally.

Our little episode in the hotel lobby was not finished, however. What followed was an exercise in humility. Not only did they bill us the equivalent of a night's lodging just to clean a measly load of wash, they lost our socks and underwear.

"Has anybody seen these guys' underwear?" the hotel clerk announced loudly to a group of staff and visitors. Sheez. We blushed and tried to act nonchalant while hotel clerks asked each other boisterously, "Has anybody seen these guys' underwear?"

Eventually, a hotel manager retrieved our elusive gear from his office — heaven only knows what it was doing in there — and we proceeded to pack our bags ▶

You may see it in the Enquirer under the title The Mood of America '86, but out here on the road we have our own term for these 48-hour whistle stops....

Barnstorming America

—JIM BORGMAN

60 HALFWAY

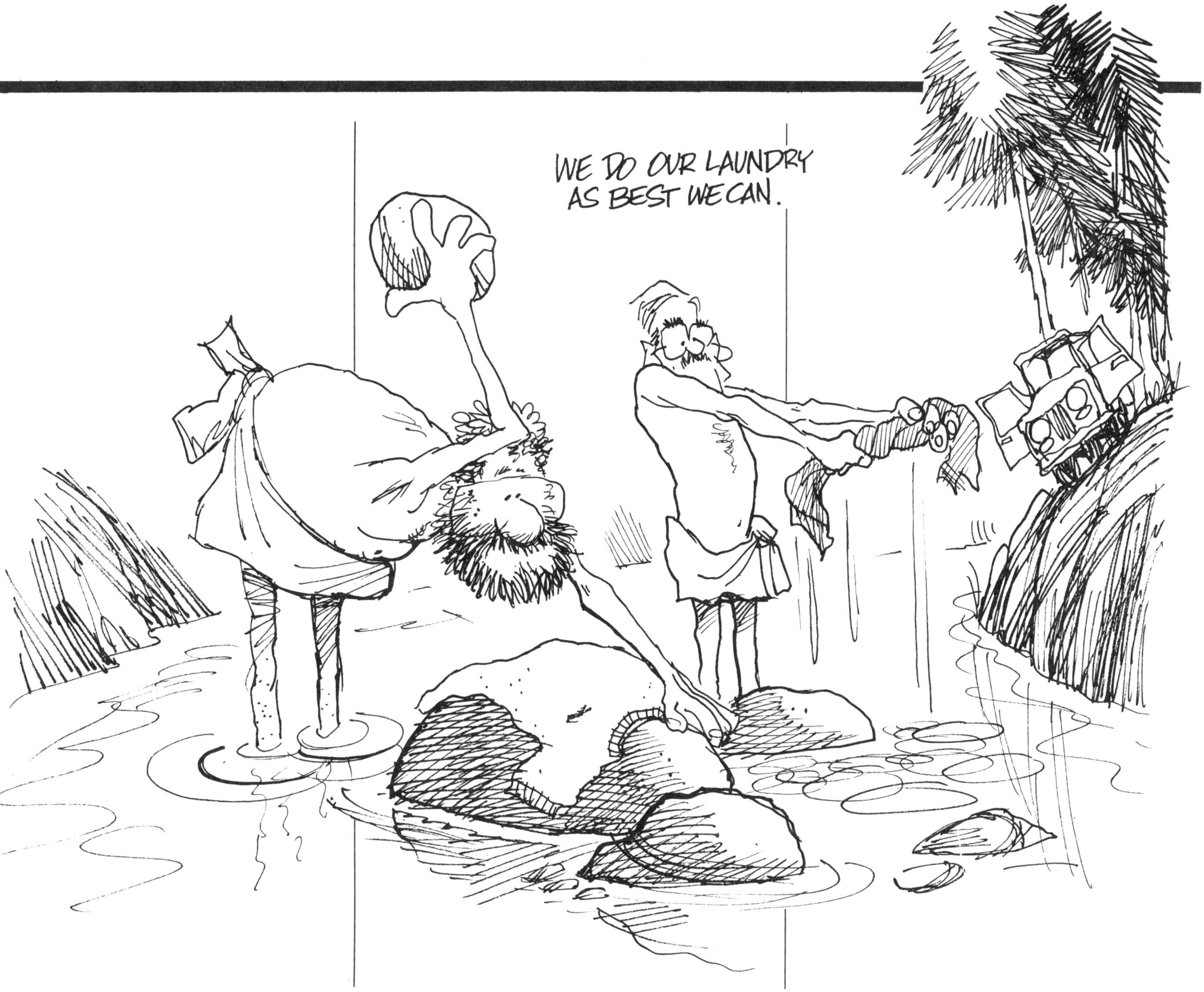
WE DO OUR LAUNDRY AS BEST WE CAN.

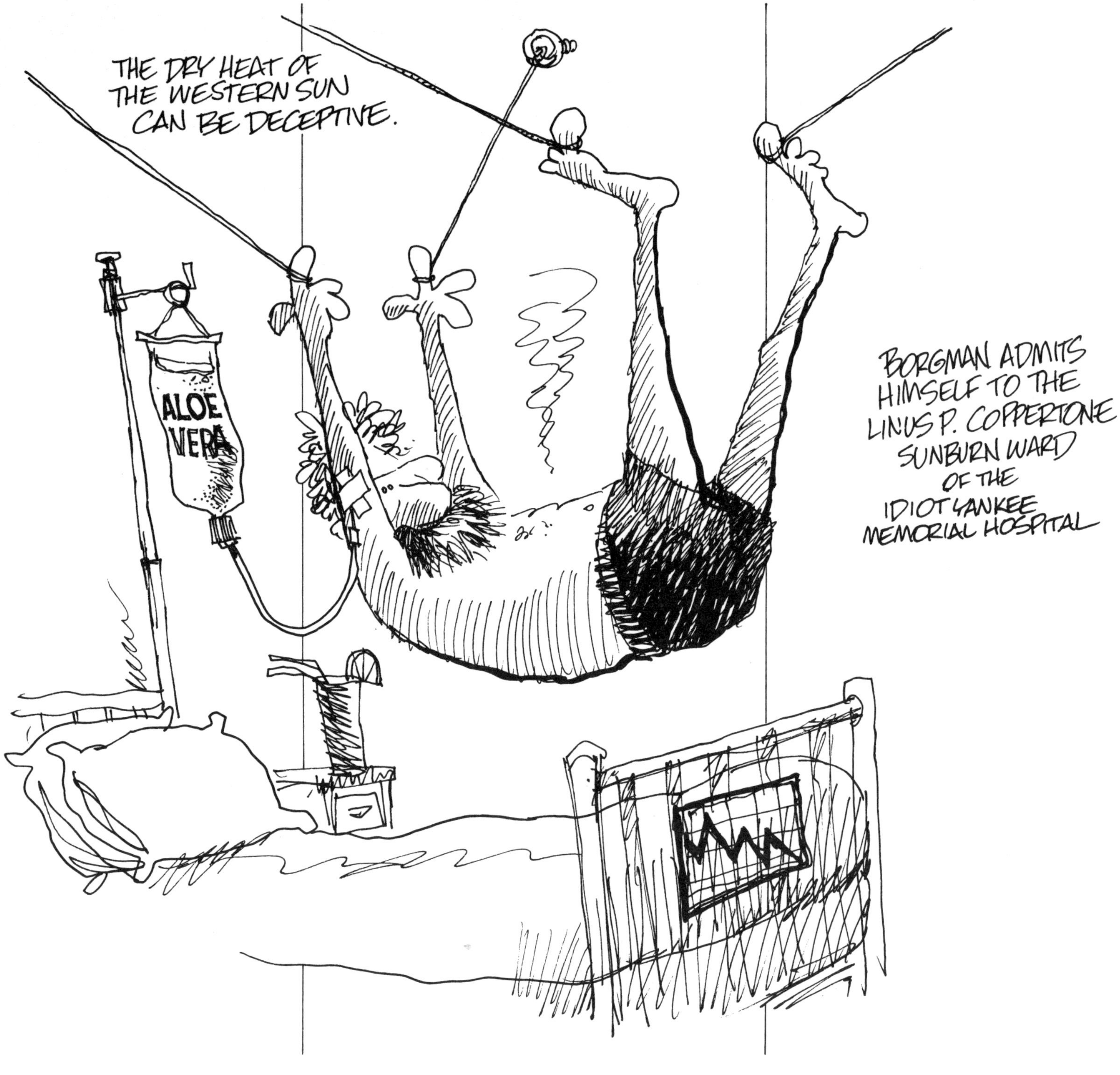
THE DRY HEAT OF
THE WESTERN SUN
CAN BE DECEPTIVE.
ALOE
VERA
BORGMAN ADMITS
HIMSELF TO THE
LINUS P. COPPERTONE
SUNBURN WARD
OF THE
IDIOT YANKEE
MEMORIAL HOSPITAL

IF OUR HOTEL ROOM HAS THE WRONG KIND OF TELEPHONE HOOK UP, MCCARTY MUST IMPROVISE TO TRANSMIT HIS STORIES BACK TO CINCINNATI.

ON THE VINE STREET END, COMPUTER WIZARD JOHN BRYAN TELLS US WHETHER THE MAGIC WORKED.

"YEAH, YOUR STORY GOT HERE, BUT SOMEBODY LOST IT..."

AFTER AWHILE YOU LEARN HOW TO SLEEP ON PLANES.

as tactfully as is possible in a hotel parking lot.

All our days on this monthlong barnstorming tour of America haven't been as eventful, but they haven't been boring either. With two weeks of travel under our belts, we've been through 11 states, taken 11 flights, changed time zones 11 times, put almost 2,000 miles on nine rental cars and seen a larger variety of sights across the country than many people see in a lifetime.

We've developed a complicated routine of rising early, working fast and retiring late. All this is made less troublesome by a few simple conveniences we've come to cherish: a good shower head, a scan feature on the car radio, a hotel room phone with a removable cord to ease electronic story transmission, firm mattresses and a pair of good desks.

Waking after only a couple hours of sleep is made easier by a symphony of alarm clocks in the morning. I have a watch that beeps at a high pitch and a battery-operated travel alarm that chirps about the same time Borgman's wind-up alarm is ringing off the night stand.

A few tips from Charles Kuralt, who has dozed in his share of fleabag dwellings while "On the Road" for CBS News for the last decade and a half, has made sleeping in different motel beds every night easier.

Never sleep on the side of the bed next to the telephone table, Kuralt says, although that is where you're inclined to sleep because it will be easier to answer your morning wake-up call.

"Ah," Kuralt cautions, "but that's what every milk-fed, corn-fattened, 250-pound traveling salesman from Dubuque figures, too. That's where he sleeps, and that's where he sits to make his phone calls to the home office. So the side of the mattress next to the telephone table is broken down, and you spend the night at a perilous angle, your slumber lost to the necessity of keeping a tight grip on the uphill sheets to keep from falling onto the floor."

We've tingled our taste buds during the trip with local culinary specialties whenever possible. This includes some of the best barbequed pork ever tasted in Fort Worth, Texas, pot roast in Salt Lake City, Utah, salmon in Washington and California, and Mexican food in San Diego, Calif., and Denver. This we've washed down with local brews of Lone Star in Texas and Rainier in Washington.

There are still some good deals out there, too. In Dixon, Ill., a dime still buys a cup of coffee, and a nickel still gets you an hour at a downtown parking meter. Compare that to $7.10, plus tax and tip for a ▶

"YOU MISSED MILWAUKEE."

ON A BARNSTORMING TRIP LIKE THIS, EVEN A CATNAP WILL COST YOU.

FOR THOSE WHO HAVEN'T TRAVELED A LOT, THERE'S A CERTAIN THRILL IN SEEING EXOTIC NEW PLACES ON GREEN HIGHWAY SIGNS.

CLICK

Pocatello

HALFWAY 65

pot of coffee at the Hyatt in Fort Worth, Texas, or $5.25 a day for parking at the same place.

Two and a half bucks at Hada's Diner in Dixon brought a plateful of lasagna with all the fixings. A plate full of nachos, burritos, enchiladas and tacos for two at a popular Mexican eatery in San Diego cost us a bellyache and more than $60.

You'll also want to remember your wallet when you visit the Dallas-Fort Worth International Airport. They charge 50 cents an hour to drive into the airport whether you park or not. Entry to Whiteside County Field near Dixon, like most airports, is free.

Laundry aside, in Memphis and at each of our previous whistle stops, the basic friendliness of Americans has superseded any other impressions we

MCCARTY PURSUES HIS BIRDWATCHING ACTIVITIES

IT IS EASY TO START GETTING CASUAL ABOUT CATCHING PLANES

66 HALFWAY

have gathered. Scenery and climate may change from state to state, but people everywhere have been remarkably cordial.

We've put together a list of some of our favorite, and least favorite, people, places and things.

- Worst tourist trap: Graceland, Memphis — $11.95 per person, plus $1 for parking, for a rushed look at a lifetime's collection of tackiness. Also bad — Billy Bob's, Fort Worth.
- Best tourist trap: Mount St. Helens, Washington — unbelievable destruction amid indescribable beauty.
- Best restaurant: Ruth's Diner, Salt Lake City. Like eating dinner at mom's in the mountains.
- Worst restaurant: Concession stand, Mile High Stadium, Denver. Bush league fare at major league prices.
- Best dive: Pete Riscky's Barbeque, Fort Worth. Good 'n' greasy.
- Worst dive: Campbell's Famous Barbeque, Tunica, Miss. Call the life squad.
- Best scenery: Mount Rainier National Park, Washington. Also nice, drive on Missouri Route 79 along the Mississippi River.
- Best deal: A Denver Zephyrs baseball game. Five bucks for second-row seats and a good show.
- Worst deal: A load of laundry for $63 at the Memphis Sheraton Hotel.
- Harshest living: Tonto National Forest, Arizona — 115 degrees in the shade, if you can find any. Only fit for lizards and buzzards.
- Biggest surprise: A rattlesnake in the Arizona desert.
- Worst disappointment: Swimming in the Great Salt Lake.
- Worst substance abuse: Cocaine — a zonked-out woman in Venice, Calif., who spent 15 minutes talking on a pay phone that was out of order; beer — Royal Andrews, of Packwood, Wash., who claims to drink a half a case a night; coffee — Borgman and McCarty.
- Most elusive prey: The armadillo. ■

Tunica, Mississippi

Condemned shacks on Sugar Ditch

Tunica, Mississippi

—Jim Borgman

He might be a king on a throne, the way Sonny Lowery sits so proud and content on his rickety wooden chair in the shade of a willow on the oppressive 102-degree day.

"I don't have nothing else to do all day except sit right here in the shade," says Lowery, pleased as can be.

Pretty soon along comes George Shannon, a carpenter from down the road. Shannon pulls up in his rusty green pickup, spits a long shot of tobacco juice onto the blacktop and asks whether anyone wants to go trolling for catfish with him in the Mississippi River.

Lowery says forget it.

"I been baptized one time, and one time is enough. I don't go out on no boats, and I never learned how to swim," he says. "That's why I put two showers in the house — I don't even like water in a bathtub."

O.C. White, the best bricklayer in Tunica, went fishing last week and look what it got him — drowned. Fell overboard pulling up his net. His boots filled with water, dragged him under for good.

Lowery figures that he's one of the luckiest guys in town, no reason to tempt fate by changing now. To his left stands his castle, a one-story home built with his own hands, clearly the finest home on the block.

"Drove every nail in myself," he proclaims proudly.

To his right he parks his coach, an Electra 225. Beyond stretches his kingdom, the Sunrise Subdivision.

As good a life as Lowery lives, statistics say he lives in poverty, which in Tunica County, the poorest county per capita in the country, isn't such a bad lot. Lowery, 50, a married father of eight, is poor in a place where being just plain poor can actually be an attractive proposition. A family of four with an income less than $10,609 is considered poor in the United States. Lowery, whose household now numbers seven, would need to earn $15,500 to escape poverty.

Poverty comes in degrees in Tunica, where 45 percent live below the poverty level, and the median household income is $6,600 a year. There is a level of poor that encompasses people like Lowery and most of his neighbors in Sunrise Subdivision. Then there is what people call "Dirt Poor," a large number that ▶

SONNY LOWERY
SUNRISE SUBDIVISION
TUNICA, MISSISSIPPI

MISSISSIPPI 69

SONNY LOWERY
TUNICA, MISSISSIPPI

includes big families like the 12 Browns, who live in a shack on the town's north side.

At the bottom are the "Sugar Ditch Alley Poor," a category of particular repute named especially for the former and present residents of a section of Tunica so depressed that Jesse Jackson called it "America's Ethiopia" during a visit in the summer of 1985.

Hosey Fleming is one of a handful of holdouts who stayed behind to live in the Ditch after the government condemned and evacuated it. His home is a two-room shack without plumbing, stove or electricity. He uses an oil lamp for light, a battery-powered radio for entertainment.

"I don't have any problems with roaches or mice 'cause I ain't got no food," says Fleming, 35, who has no job or prospects of finding one. Sometimes he stays with a girlfriend, one of about two dozen former residents of the Ditch whom the government relocated in new house trailers about a mile away.

"They all said they didn't know it was so bad back there, but it really was. Every time it rained, the ditch overflowed," Fleming said.

The Sugar Ditch was a sweet name for an open sewer that ran behind rows of dilapidated shacks occupied almost exclusively by blacks. The shacks were hidden from view by whites' stately homes with large pillared porches, by lush magnolia and mimosa trees, by buildings in the town's central business district and by the First Baptist Church.

"Here was this big white folks' church right in the middle of it for all those years, and they never did anything about it," Lowery said. "I don't know how the people lived in those conditions for so long. I would have gotten out of there. But I guess most of them were on welfare and had no other choice.

"It made the whole town look so bad when the news came out last summer," Lowery said, recalling the wide media coverage given Jesse Jackson's visit to the Ditch.

Next to Lowery's, Bessie Rudd, who moved to Tunica 10 years ago, operates a beauty salon out of her home. A mother of six boys and a girl, Rudd is studying cosmetology in hope that she'll be able to teach it next year at the local high school.

"I didn't even know there was a Sugar Ditch until it came on the news. It's not just me either. A lot of people said they didn't know about it," she said.

Nor did many of Tunica's whites claim to know the degree of poverty existing in their own back yard.

"In this part of the country there's poor just like everywhere else," says Willie Ainsworth, a white from nearby Clarksdale who sells watermelons from the

HOSEY FLEMING
SUGAR DITCH RESIDENT,
IN THE SHADE OF HIS GIRLFRIEND'S
TRAILER — TUNICA, MISS.

BESSIE RUDD
RUDD BEAUTY SALON
TUNICA, MISSISSIPPI

back of his pickup in the black neighborhoods of Tunica.

That kind of reaction is typical of the turf, according to Hodding Carter III, a Mississippian who served in the State Department during the administration of Jimmy Carter.

He wrote that many southern whites "live on the incredible fiction that they don't have poverty all around them. It's an elaborate edifice you have to maintain if you want to live with yourself."

Lowery could write a history on life in the South. He was reared on a plantation near Jackson, Miss., on the fertile river delta. He worked first as a cotton picker and later as a tractor driver and field boss before the landowner shot himself in the head. "I went to get him a cup of coffee, and the next thing I know they're telling me he's dead."

On Sept. 14, 1951, he moved to Tunica. "I remember the exact date because I came in toting bags of cotton on a mule," says Lowery, whose given name is Elliseara.

He remembers when racial segregation was a way ▶

Alice Brown watches the children while other family members chop cotton in Tunica, Mississippi. Twelve people share the cinderblock house.

72 MISSISSIPPI

FIELD WORKERS, TUNICA, MISSISSIPPI

of life, when there were separate doors for blacks and whites, separate public drinking fountains and no seats for blacks at the bus station. Not only did he survive those days, he prospered.

"I don't know what I did right raising my kids, but none of them have ever been arrested or put in jail, none of them are on dope, nothing. I guess I better knock on wood. I've been lucky," says Lowery.

Two of Lowery's daughters and a son moved to Chicago to find work — the girls work at a hotel, the boy at a Taco Bell. They aren't alone. In the last 25 years, Tunica County's population has declined by half to about 9,600, reflecting a massive loss of farm jobs. Most, like the Lowery children, left for Northern industrial cities.

Some residents don't think the depressed employment should temper the easy-going pace of life in Tunica.

"This is a peaceful town, really," Rudd says, "there just aren't any jobs here."

She moved to Memphis for two years to improve her business but couldn't wait to return to Tunica.

"My mom lives in an apartment in Memphis, and she doesn't even have a restroom. There's bad conditions everywhere," Rudd said. "And my children are happier here. They didn't like all the noise in the city. They like the peace and quiet of the schools here."

Rudd would have a hard time convincing Alice Brown that Tunica is peaceful. During the day while her father works on a road crew and her mother picks cotton, Brown, 23, watches over eight young brothers, sisters, nieces and nephews.

"It's bad down here. There's a lot of drunks and dope — you ought to be here on the weekend when they come racing down the road wrecking their cars. There's rapes and break-ins and fights, too."

Brown lives on the north side of Tunica, the opposite end of town from the relative peace found by Lowery and Rudd in the Sunrise Sub.

She suspects the relocated Sugar Ditch residents who live across the street in the new trailers — while she and 11 other Browns share a cinder block and tin roof shack — are better off financially than they appear.

"We're the real poor people," she said. "Some of those people from down there in Sugar Ditch, they got money they just don't want to give it up."

Ainsworth figures the poor blacks of Tunica are getting what they deserve. He says he can count on selling anywhere from 30 to 100 watermelons a day — more after the first of each month once the government assistance checks arrive.

"There's a bunch of people down here who don't give a damn. They're lazy, and they won't get up off their butts," he said. "They think that because of what happened years ago, the white man owes them something. But heck, I think it's all been kind of turned around now."

If the poor of Tunica don't work, it's not because they prefer the government's money. Mississippi's welfare dole is the lowest in the United States. ∎

MISSISSIPPI 73

WATERMELON SALESMAN
WILLIE AINSWORTH
TUNICA, MISSISSIPPI

SUNRISE SUBDIVISION
TUNICA, MISSISSIPPI

Memphis, Tennessee

ELVIS GRAVESITE - MEDITATION GARDEN, GRACELAND

Most big-name stars get a mayor's proclamation and a mention in the *World Almanac* when they die. A small shrine at most.

Elvis Presley was so big that when he died in 1977, they dedicated an entire museum in his honor: Graceland.

But as museums go, this one is strictly bush league. Don't expect to stroll around Graceland as if it's the Smithsonian. A visit here is akin to stopping for lunch at any of the myriad of fast-food restaurants that line Elvis Presley Boulevard — quick and unsatisfying.

Once you pass through the front gate of wrought iron musical notes, grab your hat and hold on tight.

"Welcome to Graceland. Park here. Wait here. Buy your tickets here. Enter the shuttle bus here. No video or flash cameras please. Walk over here. Follow me please. Come over here. Go over there. I said no flash cameras, sir. Enter the shuttle bus over there. Did everyone have a good time?"

Whew. Like, "Don't Be Cruel (to a Heart That's True)."

Before you know it, the tour is over, you're out $11.95 a head, $8.25 for children, and you haven't learned one thing about Elvis that you didn't already know.

Forty-five minutes of this runaround is enough to make you moo in protest, the way they herd groups like cattle from one guide to the next. Guides stand at designated Graceland stations, delivering the same spiel about 100 times a day until they start to sound like a chorus of parrots.

"I could have stayed in there for four more hours," said Robin Beeson of Muncie, Ind. "I wish they wouldn't have rushed us so much. We'll probably come back again before we leave for home to catch what we missed."

Don't dare try to slow things down to read some original Elvis lyrics, study a favorite Elvis gold record or just reminisce about the first time you saw Elvis twist his hips and make the girls swoon. No time, tour group, have to hurry onward into the abyss of wealth.

Graceland is probably the largest collection of expensive junk ever assembled under one roof — a ▶

Great Schlock Items:

STOLEN FROM THE HEARTBREAK HOTEL
$3.95 SUCH A DEAL

FURRY BLUE ELVIS SLIPPERS SELL FOR $19.95 PAIR

(HIS HEAD IS WHERE THE BUNNY WOULD BE)

REVOLVING 'LOVE ME TENDER' MUSIC BOX $14.95

testimonial to the tackiness that money can buy.

Three thousand people a day scuttle through the mansion Elvis bought for $100,000 in 1957. His daughter Lisa, 18, will inherit Graceland when she turns 25.

On the first floor is a gold-leaf grand piano worth $500,000, stained-glass peacocks and walls covered entirely by mirrors because Elvis thought they made the house look more spacious. Most rooms have television sets because, in addition to his more celebrated addictions, we learn from our tour guide that Elvis also was hooked on the tube.

In Graceland's basement is Elvis' famous TV lounge where he liked to watch sports on three sets simultaneously. The tour guide wouldn't say which of the sets were replacement models for the ones Elvis destroyed with blasts from his trusty .45.

Next door is the pool room where Elvis liked to

listen to gospel music and play eight ball or rotation.

"Elvis loved pool, and from what we hear, he was pretty good at it," the guide reveals. Interesting. Did she glean that juicy tidbit from *Elvis and Me* by his ex-wife, Priscilla?

Around the corner is Elvis' Jungle Room, which he decorated in early Hawaiian with furniture constructed of wood carved in the shape of animal heads, mattresses covered with fur and a veritable jungle of imitation tropical plants and antlers.

The upstairs is closed to the public because that's where Elvis' aunt Delta Biggs lives, according to provisions of his will.

Outside the mansion are some of Elvis' favorite cars: a Ferrari he liked to drive around Memphis at 165 mph, a 1955 pink Cadillac, a pink Jeep and a couple of black Stutz Blackhawks that start with a solid gold key.

Possibly the two most interesting stops on the Graceland tour are the Trophy Room and Racquetball Building on the grounds at the rear of the mansion. But here again, it's rush, rush, rush.

The Trophy Room is jammed with memorabilia. There are walls of gold records, proclamations and trophies, 50,000 petitions from teen-age girls calling for Elvis' exemption from military service, racks of gaudy fringe-and-rhinestone stage costumes, size 12D shoes and piles of jewelry emblazoned with "TCB" for "Taking Care of Business," his motto. On display are the three Grammy awards won by the king of rock 'n' roll, all for gospel records. To believe the photographs in the Trophy Room, you'd think Elvis was forever slim and young.

The Racquetball Building is where Elvis spent his last morning, Aug. 16, 1977, exercising and playing the piano. "Blue Eyes Crying in the Rain" and "Unchained Melody" were the last songs he sang.

Only at Elvis' grave do the guides allow you time to stop, rest and meditate. But by that time, you're out of air-conditioned comfort and sweltering in heat and air so thick you practically have to slice it to breathe.

Elvis fans are special, though. These are people who stood by Elvis after he died, as his public image disintegrated and his addiction to drugs became known. It would take more than a little rough treatment to sour their love for this native of Tupelo, Miss., who changed the music world forever with his blend of black rhythm-and-blues into a new sound called rock 'n' roll.

"I liked the feeling he put into his songs. It felt just like he was singing to me," said Joyce Short of Bostic, N.C., who was here on her honeymoon. "I remember the day he died. It was like a part of me was gone."

Short was able to keep her composure at the tomb, but a few steps away, Patty Severs let her emotions get the better of her. Tears streamed down her cheeks from behind her sunglasses.

"OK, just a minute, I'll be all right. OK. This is embarrassing. I do this at every funeral, too," said Severs, who drove 12 hours from Dumont, Iowa, just to visit Graceland. Her husband and children waited in the wings, fidgeting, their eyes skyward, feigning perplexity.

"I guess the thing that upsets me most about this place is that they don't seem to appreciate Elvis as a human being, only as an entertainer. And that's what killed him, all the demands and the pressure of always having to be the best," Severs said.

She may be right. During his last year alive, Elvis played 107 concerts in 80 cities despite being plagued by glaucoma, diabetes, hypertension, drug addiction and an enlarged heart.

Severs, 34, asks one favor of her family: When she dies, they must promise to place her beloved Elvis scrapbook in the casket with her.

Daughter Tracy said that she would comply with her mother's strange request but that she had devised a scheme of her own.

"If Madonna dies, I swear I'm dragging her to see Madonna's house," Tracy, 15, said with a smirk.

Robin Beeson, 20, and a friend, Mindy Myers, 19, said they started planning their excursion to Graceland before Christmas.

"I'm into nostalgia. I guess I would rather have lived in the '50s, except if I did, I'd be old right now," Beeson said.

"Mindy and I will sit there for hours and listen to Elvis music, and my mom and dad can't believe it. No heavy metal for us — Elvis and Judas Priest just don't mix."

Myers said she thought Elvis was sexy, provided that you skip 1962-1968 and 1974 until he died. "Bless his heart, I still love him, but he looked horrible then."

The tour isn't finished after you leave Graceland. The shuttle bus drops you off across the street at a retail complex of Elvis souvenir stores, Elvis record and tape shops and his former touring jets and bus.

"If he were alive and came back, he'd never believe this," said Mrs. Robert Louis Stevenson of Lansing, Ill. "He would think this is ridiculous, I think."

If Elvis did come back, he might want to buy his own personalized bottle of "Love Me Tender" conditioning shampoo for $4.99 or a $19.95 pair of fuzzy blue slippers with a plastic bust of The King where the big toe goes.

"No, we don't sell many of those," said sales clerk Sylvia Boone, referring to the slippers. "Mostly beach towels, coffee mugs, bells — that's about it, really."

As ridiculous as the business of marketing post-mortem Elvis has become, Stevenson, a 58-year-old grandmother, counts herself among the people for whom the image of Elvis will never fade.

"I was one of those parents who thought those sexual gyrations of Elvis' were ridiculous. But my daughter fell in love with him. Now my husband and I understand what all the kids were wild about. He was great, and I have to admit that on the day he died, my daughter and I cried together." ■

Hannibal, Missouri

Mark Twain called it St. Petersburg in *The Adventures of Tom Sawyer.*

The storybook setting of youthful adventure was actually Hannibal, just a bend in the Mississippi River really, about 100 miles upriver from St. Louis. But what a magical town it was when put to words by native son Samuel Langhorne Clemens, better known as Mark Twain.

What red-blooded American boy or girl wouldn't die to be Tom Sawyer, Becky Thatcher or Huckleberry Finn exploring the labyrinth of deep caves outside Hannibal where fugitives like Injun Joe once hid?

Who wouldn't dream of strapping logs together for a raft to sail to uninhabited Jackson Island or just drift wherever the current takes you? You had to admire Tom and Huck's mettle, crawling out their bedroom windows at night in search of excitement or pouring castor oil down a crack in the floorboard.

The best part about Twain's wonderful world of fiction is that his characters were based on real people, and many of the places they visited still exist around Hannibal today.

Tom was in reality young Sam Clemens, who as a boy really did whitewash a fence, get lost in a cave, skip school and swim in the river. Clemens' mother was Aunt Polly; his brother and sister were cousins Sid and Mary.

Huck was Tom Blankenship, a ragamuffin who lived on North Street behind Clemens' boyhood home. Becky was Laura Hawkins, who lived on Hill Street across from the Clemenses next to Grant's Drug Store and who later moved to Cincinnati. Others, such as Injun Joe and Jim, an escaped slave, also were based on real people.

In a town steeped in such legend, you wonder how Hannibal's youth of today feel about their celebrated predecessors. Do boys and girls in Hannibal enjoy life

HANNIBAL REVISITED 1986

ALIEN STEAMBOAT DESTROYER

80 MISSOURI

with the same zest as Tom and Huck and Becky? Do they paint fences? Explore caves? Camp on islands? Play hooky? Cool off in the river? Roam through graveyards?

"I mostly ride my bike," says Wes Caldwell, 17, seated on his dirt bike with wide, studded tires and high handlebars. He is wearing a heavy metal T-shirt and an earring. "I like to go to the teen center, listen to music, dance, play pool, play video games."

About Twain — have you ever read *Huckleberry Finn?* "Nope." *Tom Sawyer?* "Yeah, maybe." *The Prince and the Pauper?* "What?" *Roughing It?* "Never heard of it." "The Jumping Frog of Calaveras County"? "I heard of that one."

The central business district teemed with tourists but seemed devoid of local youth. Nearly all of the town's youngsters were swimming at the Hannibal Community Pool. As Caldwell pedaled away, others emerged from the fenced-in oasis.

"I like baseball and football best," said Chris Koppitz, 12, who professes a fascination for a cave nearby, now called Mark Twain Cave. He has been there five times. But he's not too familiar with Twain's work.

"It's really kind of surprising," he said. "Here we are living in Hannibal, and people expect us to know all about Mark Twain, but we don't."

"I'm not the reading type," pipes in Chris' 13-year-old brother, Bryan.

And Marvin Ward, 12, a graduate of Mark Twain Elementary School, says, "I wouldn't get in that river if you paid me."

This train of conversation went on for a while — their responses presenting a depressing pattern.

How could this be? Twain's Hannibal was a land of wonder, an adolescent Eden in the days before Kings Island or Disney World, a town so marvelous that Twain's readers could only dream of such a place.

What has Twain's world come to — a legion of Pac-Man wizards without regard for the folklore of their home?

Just as you're ready to give up, disillusioned by a ▶

new generation of Hannibal youth, along come Tom and Huck reborn in Jams and high-topped tennis shoes.

"I like playing baseball and swimming, mostly. I earn money cutting grass," said Stewart McIntyre, 12, who for the sake of this story we'll call Tom Sawyer — a character he began reading about this summer on his own, "just for fun."

Last year, Stewart finished third in a race to find out who could whitewash a picket fence the fastest in town. This year, he plans to enter raft races on the river and catch a frog to enter in a frog-jumping contest. He has been to Mark Twain Cave four times and said he discovered something new every time.

"It's such a little town, but people from all over the world come to visit, which I think is pretty neat," Stewart said.

Huck, alias George Clayton, 12, is a classic Twain character.

"I think it would have been fun to live back then, to play hooky, explore the caves, dip the girls' pigtails in ink," he said.

George has updated that old Twain script. He chases girls around the pool, pushes them in the water, snaps the straps of their bikini tops, that sort of thing.

"We don't have a swimming hole so we do the best we can here," George said.

Of course, our trio wouldn't be complete without Becky Thatcher. That would be Shannon Fohey, 12.

"I want to try out for Becky Thatcher next year when I'm old enough," Shannon said.

Each year around the Fourth of July during Hannibal's Tom Sawyer Days, seventh-grade boys and girls dress up in the clothing of Twain's characters, meet with tourists at the various Mark Twain landmarks, write essays and give speeches in competition for the best Tom and Becky in town. Winners receive prizes, greet visiting dignitaries on riverboats and earn a trip to St. Louis.

Shannon should be a shoo-in for next year's Becky Thatcher. She's already well-acquainted with Huck Finn and the kind of mischief Becky had to contend with.

"I was one of the girls he pushed in the pool today," she says shyly. ■

MISSOURI 83

84 MISSOURI

INJUN JOE HANGS OUT
AT THE
MARK TWAIN DINETTE
HANNIBAL, MO.

Miami, Florida

Everglades Vice

Alligators and Johnny Tigertail have a mutual understanding: Johnny will feed them a daily helping of fish and chicken as long as they continue to lurk in the swamps that surround the Miccosukee Indian village where Johnny lives.

But that's as far as the agreement goes. There is no guarantee that if Johnny tries to catch one of the big, sharp-toothed reptiles — which happens to be this 9-year-old's favorite sport — they won't try to bite off a finger or a foot or more.

"It's kind of fun to catch them, but it's dangerous. Sometimes they'll get your hand in their mouth, and they won't let go," says Johnny, speaking about alligators the way a Midwesterner his age might talk about spiders and snakes. Except parents in the Midwest don't have to worry about spiders and snakes devouring their children.

"When they bite, they try to twist it off. That's what they did to me here," he says, proudly holding up a scarred hand to display his latest wound.

Living among the alligators and other wild inhabitants of the Everglades has been a way of life for the Miccosukee Indians since before Florida became a state in 1819. The Indians hunted the Everglade swamps in cypress log canoes and lived in tree islands, known as hammocks, separate from their relatives the Seminoles, who also call Florida home. The Indians that remain are descendants of a few families that escaped the government's attempt to send them to the West after the Indian Wars of the 1800s.

About 500 Miccosukees make up the tribe today. They construct crafts and clothing for sale at a general store. They operate a restaurant on the Tamiami Trail that links the east and west coasts of the state, and they run airboat rides over the Everglade swamps that are popular with tourists.

Johnny speaks the Miccosukee language as well as English. Many tribe members speak only Miccosukee.

The boy said he developed a fascination for alligators at age 3 but didn't start stalking them until a year or so later, after he fine-tuned his technique.

"I get better all the time," he said. "I'm pretty careful."

Let's hope he stays more careful than his mentor, Bobby Tiger, an old-timer who works at the Indian Culture Center on the Tamiami Trail. Tiger is missing a finger and the end joints of two others from too-close encounters with his prey.

"There are bigger gators, but mostly I go for the ones 3 feet or less," Johnny says.

By big, Johnny means man-eaters up to 14 feet long that normally stay farther out in the glades. But when ▶

FLORIDA 87

AIRBOAT RIDE IN THE EVERGLADES.

EVERGLADES, FLORIDA

88 FLORIDA

the water level recedes in the summer, the big ones come in to live in the canals at the village. That's when Johnny really has to look out.

"Most of the time I wade around in the water looking for them. You have to sneak up on them or they'll get away."

"I just like them. I don't know why."

The Everglades stretch for 5,000 square miles, saw grass and scrub trees as far as the eye can see. They remain wild and practically untouched by man except for a couple of thoroughfares and a canal that carries fresh water to quench the thirsts of crowded coastal cities.

It is a strikingly peaceful existence in contrast to life in Miami, just 20 miles to the east, a city ranked one of the worst for violent crime in the country and recognized as the drug capital of the United States. About 70% of the nation's marijuana and cocaine and 90% of its Quaaludes come through the city, according to the U.S. Drug Enforcement Administration.

The Indians and alligators share their tenuous coexistence with a practically endless array of tropical birds, reptiles, amphibians . . . and mosquitoes, billions of swarming, hungry, blood-sucking mosquitoes.

Most of the year, mosquitoes are mere pests, controllable in their small numbers. But in the summer, mosquitoes reproduce in multitudes that would boggle the mind of Einstein.

This keeps legions of birds, lizards and frogs that eat the mosquitoes happy but keeps all but the toughest tourists a safe distance away.

Most of the tourists who visit here in the summer are tough, anyway. Others, like us, are simply ignorant. We ventured into the Long Pine Key region of Everglades National Park to hike the Anhinga and Gumbo Limbo trails dressed in shorts and T-shirts — no doubt leaving smartly clothed park rangers snickering in our wake.

We lasted about 10 minutes. The mosquitoes descended on the two large pieces of fresh meat like massive squadrons of kamikaze pilots, leaving few uncovered areas unprobed. We cast cursory glances at a few turtles, herons and alligators on the trail and scrambled back to the car, scratching and itching the entire drive out of the park.

A Miccosukee Indian airboat ride earlier in the day was a far more enjoyable way to see the Everglades in the summer.

The broad flat boat with room for about 15 is propelled by a huge fan, allowing it to skim across the swampy grasslands at a velocity reminiscent of flight. There were no trees, rocks or logs on the water's surface to get in the way, so the boat went wherever the daring pilot chose to steer it. All the while pieces of grass and splashes of water flew over our heads.

But don't forget to use the cotton the Indians provide. The bare, unmuffled airboat engines are earsplitting.

In their own way, the airboats play a role in helping nature. The paths the boats clear through the saw grass uncover water for the endangered snail kite, a black hook-billed hawk found primarily in the Everglades.

Uncovered water is important to the kites because it helps them to spot the apple snails, which they feed on exclusively.

We spotted five kites and an osprey on our half-hour ride through the glades. And we spotted a couple of small alligators that managed to escape Johnny Tigertail's fearless grasp. ■

CARRIED AWAY BY MOSQUITOES IN THE EVERGLADES

FLAGLER KENNEL CLUB MIAMI, FLORIDA

McCARTY AND BORGMAN SPEND A MIAMI EVENING AT THE DOG TRACK.

90 FLORIDA

THE COMPETING DOGS ARE PARADED OUT BEFORE EACH RACE TO BE STUDIED BEFORE THE BETS GO DOWN.

EIGHT SLEEK GREYHOUNDS PER RACE, THIRTEEN RACES PER EVENING, RINGED BY ROYAL PALMS AND HISPANIC CHEERING IN THE HUMID FLORIDA BREEZE.

FLORIDA 91

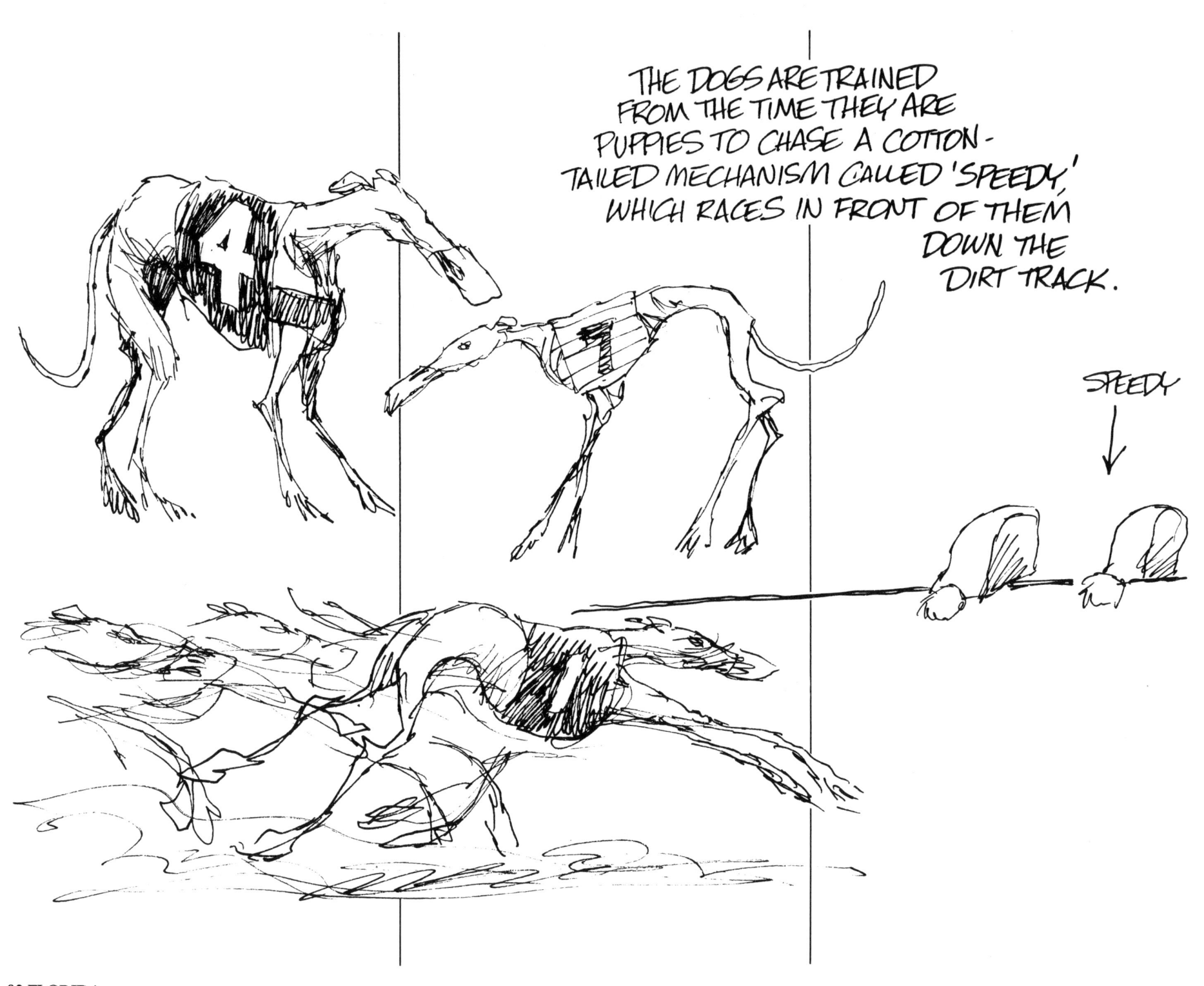

THE DOGS ARE TRAINED FROM THE TIME THEY ARE PUPPIES TO CHASE A COTTON-TAILED MECHANISM CALLED 'SPEEDY,' WHICH RACES IN FRONT OF THEM DOWN THE DIRT TRACK.

SPEEDY ↓

WATCHING THE PEOPLE,
OF COURSE,
BEATS WATCHING THE DOGS.

REGULAR RAILBIRDS
KNOW ALL THE DOGS,
THE REPUTATIONS OF
THE TRAINERS AND
WHETHER THE TRACK
IS RUNNING FAST
OR SLOW TONIGHT.

FLORIDA 93

Gloucester, Massachusetts

When a boy is born in Gloucester and brought home for the first time, his proud parents often gather around the crib and dream.

The dreams are not always of a son growing up to become a great basketball player like the kid down the road, Larry Bird, or a great leader like Massachusetts native son, John F. Kennedy, or even a great fisherman as, no doubt, the boy's father is.

Parents have an honorable aspiration here — equal to reaching the heights of those heroes — that would set their son apart from the rest of the fishermen's sons: that he become a great greasy pole walker.

The legendary greasy pole competition is part of the three-day St. Peter's Fiesta, which features a traditional blessing of the fleet in this 300-year-old port city 40 miles north of Boston.

For those of us not raised amid greasy-pole fervor, it might be difficult to appreciate the significance of the competition. But it helps to look to the harbor, where hundreds of boats bearing full cargoes of passengers and flying multicolored banners have crowded around the pole for a ringside view of the walkers.

And look to the shore, where mobs of people unable to muster a floating seat must be content to root on their favorite walkers from afar.

And finally, look to the dock offshore where a motley group of about two dozen men in drag are bunched together arm-in-arm bellowing old Italian cheers. These, believe it or not, are the mighty pole walkers.

"Viva San Pietro, viva San Pietro, viva San Pietro," they cry out in unison. The rest of the cheers, delivered in their native tongue, are incomprehensible.

Since morning they have gathered at the St. Peter's Club, the Gloucester fishermen's traditional watering hole, quaffing mugs of ale to fortify their courage. Most are dressed in the gaudiest women's outfits imaginable, a sorry lot for sure, but the parents understand and are no less proud of their boys.

It's 5 p.m. and time for the follies to begin. On one end are the boisterous walkers; on the other end is a stick with red flags attached. In between is a wooden utility pole 30 feet long, fastened to the dock horizontal to the water and covered from end to end with thick gobs of green axle grease.

The object of the contest is to hop, shuffle, slide, skip, dance or do whatever it takes to traverse the bouncing pole and grab a flag before plummeting into the brink.

The result is a comedy of errors, funny, but nauseating to watch as walkers crunch different parts of their bodies against the pole each time they slip and fall.

The master of ceremonies sounds as if he is calling an Italian boxing match:

"Leading off, Capt. Joe 'Hard Times' Scola." "Next we have Mike 'Nobby Knees' Niacastro." "That, ladies and gentlemen, was a lesson from Paul 'Mason Man' Cardoni on how not to walk the pole." "Here's John 'The Postman' Nielo — Monday, when your letters arrive all greased up, you'll know why."

The parade continues.

Joe "The Dancing Bear" Balonti, who is wearing a pink dress and pink wig, hits the pole head first and ▶

GREASY POLE WINNER JERRY CIOLINO

GREASY POLE
ST. PETER'S FIESTA
GLOUCESTER, MASS.

people wonder whether he's still alive. He is. Jimmy Vintero, ravishing in a red cocktail dress, slides along the pole on his stomach, scraping up piles of grease as he goes, making the path to the flag a little easier for the next walker.

At last, on the group's third attempt at the pole, a mustachioed construction worker named Jerry Ciolino trots the length of the greasy path to a flag and grabs it on his way down. The horns of the boats and the cheers of the throng rise in a deafening crescendo.

Ciolino, 26, is soon joined by his beat-up compatriots who leap from the dock into the water around him. Then all swim to shore where they are engulfed by the crowd, and Ciolino is hoisted aloft, a hero.

"Viva San Pietro, viva San Pietro, viva San Pietro."

While most of Gloucester's men of the sea are toasting St. Peter and the glorious show, one is at home with his wife and children, sober and savoring their company. He bucks nearly all the old traditions around Gloucester, the busiest fishing port in the East.

"Those Italians drive me crazy," says David Borge, with few sentiments for their three days of drinking, dancing, singing and praying to St. Peter, the protector of fishermen, for the success of the coming summer's catch.

Borge, 30, is a graduate of Salem State College and the captain of his own fishing trawler, *Nomad*. He surprised his fisherman father when he decided to attend college, then defied his wishes when he followed his footsteps and became a fisherman. Today they are a two-man crew on Borge's $185,000 boat.

Borge enjoyed the fiesta when he was single, even joined the pole-walking revelry a few years back, but once was enough.

Borge wears a full, dark beard; he's muscular with big calloused hands and dressed in a pair of tattered jeans and worn work boots. For five years, Borge has made a good living catching cod, flounder and haddock in the Atlantic Ocean 200 miles from shore. He is determined not to make the same mistakes as his father.

"I grew up never seeing my father for months at a time while he was at sea," Borge says, pronouncing the word "fatha" in a thick New England accent.

"I don't see how he did it for all that time — 36 years. It's a hard life; it's crazy."

Borge is breaking away from some of the fishing traditions that led so many of his predecessors to early nautical graves. Fishing is a dangerous profession, more so even than coal mining, with a constant threat of losing a finger, an arm, an eye, or drowning. Borge doesn't plan to increase the odds.

"When the catch is sold, all the bills are paid, and there's some money in the bank, why kill yourself? The other fishermen think I'm crazy to take a week off now and then. But I'm not going to kill myself; I'm not going to live like my father did and never see my son," he said.

The Borges are a contrast in styles. The son is adept at reading computer graphs and electronic readouts to find fish and avoid snags. He fixes the boat's engine when it breaks down and snacks on bran buds. The father, Norman, 53, can mend a torn net as fast as anyone, but the technical end of the business "blows his mind." When he's hungry, he munches on Twinkies.

"My father's one hell of a worker. He's like having three men on board. But electronics is the only way you're going to make any money in this business," Borge said. "People think we just throw a net into the water and catch the fish. If it was that easy, there would be thousands of people fishing."

It is easy for a fisherman to fail. Where it used to take three days to fill a boat's hold with fish, now it takes 11 or 12. Prices for equipment are skyrocketing — $40,000 for a hydraulic winch, $65,000 a year for diesel fuel, $5,000 for an electric route plotter, $10,000 for a net — while fish prices remain stable.

Banks are foreclosing on fishermen's boat loans at a pace comparable to farmers losing their land, and insurance prices have gone through the roof, costing Borge $18,000 a year for himself and his father. A growing number of fishermen have fought back by sinking their boats to collect the insurance money. There were 80 boat sinkings in Gloucester from 1970 to 1984 and close to 50 since 1980.

Borge hopes to fish for decades to come, but he wonders whether that will be possible. Many fishermen use nets with tiny holes that catch tons of fish too small to keep. They end up dead, wasted, scooped by the bucketful back into the ocean. Other fishermen risk huge fines by catching female lobsters and scraping clumps of up to 5,000 eggs from their bellies, killing generations of lobsters for the sake of a quick buck.

"They don't understand that they're slitting their own throats," he said with a helpless look.

A few docks over from Borge's *Nomad* is Sebastian Moceri, captain of the *Andromeda*, a 53-year-old Sicilian who came to Gloucester 25 years ago. He has three sons, all of whom are in college or preparing to start. One son, Michael, is a greasy pole walker.

"None of my boys want to take my job, and I don't blame them. Education is more important. I'm gonna sell everything when I turn 60, if I can make it that long," he says in a heavy Italian accent. About 85 percent of Gloucester's fisherman are Italian. Most, like Moceri, are from Sicily.

He has just returned with some friends from gathering baskets full of prickly green sea urchins, which he calls Chinese caviar. He cuts one open with a knife, making sure not to impale the urchin's quills on his hand, and pops the orange innards into his mouth.

"It's good stuff. You take a lemon, a piece of bread, a basket of urchins and a jug of wine, sit on the rocks, it's just like a picnic.

"But my kids don't like them. You know, American born," Moceri says with a wink. ■

DAVID BORGE
FISHERMAN
GLOUCESTER, MASS.

MASSACHUSETTS 97

DAVID BORGE
AT THE FISH HOLE
ON THE NOMAD.

Cruising with Humpbacks

Our first sighting came off the bow about 10 a.m.

"Thar she blows," someone called, flippantly using the timeless cry of whale hunters.

The pilot of the *Privateer II* turned the boat several degrees east, gunned the engines and headed toward the spout, a short, full spray of water that identified the humpback whale. Armed with cameras and binoculars, we strained in anticipation of a maiden sighting for most of us aboard — a whale in the wild.

The water spout, it turned out, came from a pair of whales, a mother humpback and her young calf swimming in tandem alongside our boat.

This adult whale's tail, known as a fluke, was mottled with blotches of white and black, which told our guides we were observing a humpback named Falco and her calf.

The whales seemed to have no fear of our boat as they glided through the rough water and surfaced for air wherever they chose. They appeared to be slow, lumbering mammals, but it was an illusion caused by their size. Humpbacks can grow to 40 feet and weigh 40 tons.

We were able to catch only a few glimpses of one whale — a finback that can weigh up to 65 tons and can reach lengths of 70 feet. It's known as the greyhound of the sea because of its speed. True to form, after our first spotting of a finback's telltale tall, thin water spout, our boat sped to the spot where it submerged. When the finback re-emerged several minutes later, it was hundreds of yards away. It showed itself one more time, flipped its fluke high into the air as if to wave goodbye, then lost us.

Much more numerous and easily observable were large schools of playful, Atlantic white-sided dolphins, which followed our boat. Some skimmed effortlessly alongside our speeding craft; others rode the boat's wake and occasionally leaped out of the water to the delight of the photographers on board.

A whale watch is a difficult task for a photographer. Whales rise to the surface for air every three to five minutes, and when they emerge, they stick only enough of their bodies out of the water for a quick exhale and inhale. It's easy to see why so little is known about whales and why studying them is difficult.

Scientists are learning more from tracking whales. They know, for instance, that Falco's calf was born in the Caribbean Sea. Whales eat voraciously off the Cape Ann coast of Massachusetts, but hardly eat a thing while spending their winters in the Caribbean. Many of the whales we saw migrate 4,000 miles a year, our guide said.

Biologists working off the coast of Cape Ann have cataloged nearly 3,000 whale flukes. Each fluke is unique and used to differentiate whales just as fingerprints distinguish humans.

The same ocean conditions that make the Cape Ann area among the most bountiful of all the world's fishing waters also attract the whales. As many as 3,000 of the world's largest living creatures spend their summers here feeding on as much as a ton of fish and plankton a day.

The whales are partners in a marine ecosystem readily visible from the deck of our boat. When the whales dive deep in search of schools of tiny red shrimp known as krill, they force schools of small fish to the surface where larger fish such as bluefish and mackerel pursue them with sharp teeth. The wildly swimming fish at the surface cause a bubbly whirlpool that attracts birds such as gulls and petrels to the feast.

The *Privateer II* is one of a fleet of excursion boats that make several two-hour trips daily to Jeffrey's Ledge, where the whales feed. The ledge area, eight miles from shore, is known as the shallows, a relative term for a section of the ocean 100 feet deep.

By the end of our six-hour whale hunt, we had spotted several humpback whales, the one finback whale and the dolphins.

I climbed off the boat with a distinct feeling that I probably would never visit Sea World or any other marine amusement park again. I knew that nothing they could offer could be more entertaining than the show I had just seen. ■

Lancaster, Pennsylvania

Hours before the rooster crows, Daniel Rudolph rises in the moonlight to prepare for market. The clock on the night table reads 3:30 a.m. when Rudolph slips out of bed, being careful not to wake his wife or three young children still deep in slumber. He pulls on a pair of blue twill trousers, buttons a tan work shirt all the way to the collar and tiptoes out to the kitchen, work boots in hand. For breakfast he spoons down a big bowl of hot oatmeal.

By 4 o'clock, Rudolph is in the barn hoisting cartons filled with fresh vegetables from a huge cooler and loading them onto the back of a truck bound for the Central Market in Lancaster, a 20-minute drive from his farm in Washington Borough.

An hour later he is unloading the produce for sale, taking great care to make sure all the different vegetables are cleaned, whole and arranged attractively in their individual cartons.

The first customers start to arrive about 6 a.m. They crowd around Rudolph's vegetable stand clutching their market bags asking, "How much are the onions?" "Are your raspberries fresh?" "How much are the tomatoes?" "What are those brown marks?"

Each of Rudolph's replies comes with a smile. He doesn't have to think for more than a moment because he has answered all the questions many times before.

"Fifty cents for the small carton of onions, a dollar for the large . . . Yes, they are fresh; we grow them ourselves . . . Tomatoes are $1.50 a pound . . . We had a hail storm earlier in the season that caused the marks."

Rudolph concedes that $1.50 a pound is pretty expensive, but these aren't just any tomatoes — these are home-grown, the first of the season produced by any of the farmers with stands at the Central Market.

Some customers walk away. "I can wait," sniffs one woman. But many later return, apparently deciding that local produce at a higher price is preferable to tomatoes grown in the South selling elsewhere in the market.

"I used to feel bad when people would walk away, but when you see the same faces coming back and buying, you know that you're priced right," said Rudolph, who looks young for his 24 years.

Rudolph, like most of the farmers in Lancaster County, is a member of the Mennonite Church. ▶

ELI STOLTZFUS
AT THE FAMILY ROADSIDE STAND

BIRD-IN-HAND, PENNSYLVANIA

AS WE BEGAN TO CHOOSE A FEW SNACKS, HE SAID, 'MAKE YOURSELF AT HOME,' AND WALKED AWAY TO SUPPER.

Together with the Amish, a sect of Mennonites, they make up about 10% of the largely rural county's population.

Although their numbers are growing — about 12,000 Mennonites and 14,000 Amish live in the county — many of the younger members of the conservative congregations have begun to abandon the farm and the old ways for a more modern life in the city. There's even a term around here for those who have forsaken homesteads for row houses — "Muppies," for Mennonite Urban Professionals.

"We're kind of symbolic of a dramatic shift from a farm-based culture to a professional group," said Eugene Kraybill, a reporter for the Lancaster *Intelligencer Journal*.

Kraybill, a Mennonite, saw his first movie at age 16 and never watched television. He was raised on a potato farm in Elizabethtown with five brothers, but none of them is a farmer today. Instead, they have chosen to become a lawyer, an economics professor, a mediation specialist, a doctor and a Mennonite minister.

At Market
Lancaster, PA.

"It's a cultural base that is shifting dramatically," he said. "We no longer consider ourselves the separated people.

"All Muppies have a certain amount of cultural and religious baggage they must carry. Now they're becoming unsure whether to carry it along or dump it."

Rudolph, the son of a dairy farmer and youngest of 10 children, has a brother and sister who are Muppies. One is a building contractor, the other a teacher. Rudolph, however, is content to remain a man of the soil and likes the routine.

Tuesdays and Fridays are market days; picking, cleaning and peeling are done on Mondays and Thursdays; planting is done Wednesdays and Saturdays; and Sundays are for rest. Every member of the Rudolph family joins in preparing produce for market.

Early in the season, Rudolph sells onions, asparagus, lettuce, sugar peas and greenhouse plants; in June he sells summer squash, cucumbers, berries and early tomatoes; the bulk of his produce in July, August and September comprises lima beans, green beans, tomatoes, sweet potatoes, broccoli and cauliflower.

With only four years' experience at the stand, Rudolph can't remember the Central Market in its heyday. But Charles Long can.

For 56 years, Long has spent hours at market grinding kettles full of tangy horseradish roots and pouring the aromatic mixture into glass jars with blue and white lids. He learned the secrets of horseradish from his Uncle Frank while still in grade school.

"There's so many different things you can do with horseradish, and you can't beat it when it's fresh," said Long, 64.

He must raise his voice to be heard over the crowd and a rattly fan that blows constantly at his side, dispersing the pungent horseradish vapors that tickle your nose and make your eyes water.

Long has seen hundreds of merchants come and go from the market. They don't stay around as long as they used to, he says.

"It's all a symptom of modern times. Everyone shops at the big chain stores or at mini-marts nowadays. And they eat out more than ever before." ▶

"But the way I look at it, the people shopping here are the people who are eating right," he said.

The market offers a cornucopia of culinary delights. Up and down the aisles are different stands with tables filled with fresh and smoked meats, cheeses and fish, baked goods, candy, fruit, crafts and flowers. It's this kind of senses-tingling atmosphere that makes shopping at the market so much fun for city folk jaded by years of supermarket sprees.

Little has changed since the big, dimly lit, red brick building was constructed in 1889. Here urban and rural meet for a few hours each week. But how many shoppers take time to contemplate the sweat, toil and muscle strain it took to put the produce on the table?

A visit to farmlands in places like Washington Borough, Bird-In-Hand, Intercourse, Paradise and New Holland is like a trip back to the 17th century, when the ancestors of today's farmers arrived from Europe. They are of German, or Deutsch, heritage, not Dutch from Holland as implied by their names.

Bearded Amish and Old Order Mennonite farmers dressed in dungarees, suspenders and straw hats man the fields working teams of horses and mules, cutting and harvesting bales of alfalfa hay. Youths often guide the animals while men stack the bales.

Women in aprons and bonnets bustle to and from the kitchen where they are preparing the night's supper, or they work in the flower beds, which receive tender care. Young children, barefoot and carefree in their brightly colored overalls and dresses, frolic on scooters or wagons nearby.

Farms worked by Pennsylvania Dutch families are productive. The proof is in the numbers: In 1980, Lancaster County farmers produced $424 million worth of agricultural products, more than all of

BIRDHOUSE ON AN AMISH FARM IN BIRD-IN-HAND, PENNSYLVANIA

neighboring New Jersey, the Garden State.

Everywhere on the narrow back roads you see and hear the drab gray, horse-drawn buggies that are so much a part of the Amish image. "Clippety-cloppety," they breeze by at a brisk clip that defies the fluorescent "Slow Vehicle" warnings posted on their rear bumpers.

The Amish and Mennonites appear oblivious to the cars and tour buses filled with gawkers who have traveled to see the unusual people they have only read about or watched in the movie *Witness*.

"No, we don't mind them," said Eli Stoltzfus, an Amish farmer whose bright roadside stand is a favorite tourist stop. "It's good if the people are on the road and leave us alone and don't try to take our pictures. That's against our religion."

Stoltzfus, 28, would be a Smith anywhere else — his is the most common surname among the Amish. He is a man of few words.

"Well, have to go now, alrighty," he says, parting to milk his cows.

But he doesn't close the stand. It's open for people to admire and sample his homemade root beer, birch beer, canned fruits and vegetables, noodles, cookies, jellies and apple butter, known as lottwarrick. Customers are trusted to leave their money in a box on the counter.

If Stoltzfus and the other members of religion won't admit that they're tired of the flocks of tourists and tourist traps sprouting up around Lancaster County, Margaret Martin will.

"Tourists are taking over here. They're tearing down these beautiful old barns and putting up malls and outlets everywhere," said Martin, a 73-year-old Mennonite.

"People came in here from New York and saw all these people who looked so strange. And before you knew it, there's commercialism from one end of the county to the other," she said. ▶

PENNSYLVANIA 105

AMISH SCHOOLHOUSE

BIRD-IN-HAND, PENNSYLVANIA

Martin grew up near New Holland in a farmhouse much like the ones the Amish live in today. Her family didn't have a telephone, electricity, a car or television, and all field work was done with horses.

Although Martin cherishes the simple, unblemished landscape of the Pennsylvania Dutch country and protests any attempts to change it, through the years she has chosen to update her own image. To an outsider, her appearance is conservative: long hair braided in a bun under a white hairnet, a striped blouse, skirt and no jewelry. But she says she is among the more liberal of her religion.

"My blouse is a little too flowery for most people, and my skirt is a little too red," she said. "I've changed a lot. I used to wear a cape and ribbons on a bonnet when I was younger. But the church has changed just as fast as I have." ■

BALING ALFALFA HAY

LANCASTER, PA

New York, New York

We made it.

Here on the corner of East 41st Street and Fifth Avenue in Manhattan, we're just a couple of out-of-towners trying to blend into the crowd on the sidewalk. But in our minds, we're seasoned world travelers — a little frazzled, but giddy with the thought that we survived 15 plane flights that could have plunged from the sky, 12 rental cars that could have plummeted off cliffs and 72 meals that could have been tainted.

Blending into the crowd isn't hard. Every imaginable kind of person seems to be on the streets of this metropolis.

There are Europeans dressed in baggy shirts and shorts with backpacks studying tour maps; blacks with dreadlocks zipping in and out of traffic on bicycles; Orthodox Jews with full beards and forelocks; Asians and Africans in native dress; tourists from everywhere with cameras out, posing family members in front of monuments; and businessmen and women in pinstripes, silks and linens, hustling to and fro, paying little attention because they witness the same urban panorama every day.

The streets are filled with stretch limousines and Rolls Royces, tractor trailers, endless streams of yellow cabs and vans with graffiti covering their sides — illegible, hieroglyphical spray-painted marks, not a "Wash Me" scribbled in the dirt.

Look up and you're dwarfed by skyscrapers in all directions. Only a corridor of blue is visible between the buildings where the streets cut an open swath to the sky. You can't help thinking that this opening, too, some day will be built over.

In our opinion, there's a miracle every minute on 34th Street — and at most downtown intersections. What else could explain how taxis and trucks can drive so fast and not hit a pedestrian or two at every corner? It's clear the people who walk en masse against the "Don't Walk" signs are adept at dodging the speeding vehicles. ▶

THE CONTRASTS OF THE LAST 24 HOURS HAVE BEEN TOO GREAT FOR US TO COMPREHEND.

AT NOON WE WATCHED AMISH FARMERS BALING HAY IN A PEACEFUL PENNSYLVANIA FIELD. FIVE HOURS UP THE NEW JERSEY TURNPIKE WE CRAWLED AND ELBOWED OUR WAY INTO THE CANYONS OF MANHATTAN AMIDST HONKING, SHOUTING AND THE BLARE OF RADIOS.

THOSE FOOLHARDY ENOUGH TO DRIVE INTO MANHATTAN THIS WEEKEND LEAVE SIGNS IN THEIR PARKED CARS ADVERTISING THEIR UNWORTHINESS TO VANDALS.

We like to think all the people are here for the same reason we are — to witness and help celebrate the Liberty Weekend events — but, of course, that isn't the case.

Millions of people expected to join the relighting of the Statue of Liberty ceremonies and accompanying events are from other cities, states and countries. Native New Yorkers say they know better than to risk venturing anywhere near the statue for the next several days.

"Anyone who knows what's good for them should be on their way out of town right now," said Frank Couvares, a Brooklyn native who has come to the city from his new home in Amherst, Mass., to visit a friend.

"He's not leaving his apartment for two days. I'm leaving on the third before the crunch starts. You can see it all better on TV, anyway," Couvares said.

"It's going to be too much of a madhouse down here," said Hy Drucker of Manhattan's Lower East Side. "The streets and highways will be blocked up, and you wouldn't be able to get close enough to make it worthwhile. Plus, you have to watch out for the pickpockets. I'll enjoy it better at home on TV."

Michael Bloom of Brooklyn said, "I'm getting out of here and going on a singles' weekend to Upstate New York. It's really too bad, but the best places to see the festivities are going to be mobbed, and there's no way I was going to go over to Jersey to watch it.

"The people who live here are mostly into their own things. They have their own lives, their own problems. The only people who are really into this scene are the tourists."

Not only natives, but some of the visitors, too, have been affected by a prevailing fear that the crowds may be too large to handle.

"The general advice from all of the Americans we've spoken to is to watch it on television," said Brian Marshall of London, who is with his wife, Pat, visiting their daughter Linda.

"I think we'll go down next week to see the Tall Ships after it's quieted down a bit," he said.

"It's kind of frightening," said Diana Wall of Manhattan. "I think the people of New York are a little apprehensive about that big of an influx of people into their city. I mean, there's always the possibility of a terrorist attack or a sniper attack. I think it would be smart for New Yorkers to stay away from Lower Manhattan unless they know someone with an apartment there."

Rachelle Shells is one person who refuses to be scared away by native paranoia. Shells, a Cincinnatian from the West End, was headed for the New York Public Library to study.

"I even took a week off from school to be here, so I figured I'd better get my studying done today," said Shells, a Cincinnati Tech nutrition student.

Shells has a busy week planned with her friends: Wednesday they are going to attend amateur night at the Apollo Club; Thursday a Yankees game and Friday she was hoping one of her group could find some tickets for the fireworks.

"If they can get tickets, I'll be there. If not, we'll have to watch it on TV, I guess," Shells said.

On the steps of the library, a trio of Irish visitors with eyes wide in amazement speak of how New York, in a short time, has dashed all their preconceptions.

"It's actually much cleaner and more friendly than I thought it would be. I was expecting submachine guns and Kojak running up and down the streets," said Donal Healy, a redhead from County Kerry. "And to be honest, I was expecting it to be ungodly hot and humid. But this is actually quite nice — a good Irish day."

"It's clean and quite lovely, really," said Miriam O'Connor, an auburn-haired lass amazed by the big cars, cheap gasoline and grafitti-covered subway trains.

"I noticed all the cops are very busy up and down the street, unlike the cops in Ireland," Donal Downes said.

All are overjoyed to learn, too, that New York has a variety of Irish pubs that serve Guinness Stout on tap with a big, frothy head, just like back home.

WE ARRIVE IN NEW YORK CITY WITH A SPECIAL APPRECIATION FOR THE ELLIS ISLAND IMMIGRANTS: HAVING TRAVELED THOUSANDS OF MILES TO THIS TEEMING LAND, DIRTY, TIRED AND CARRYING EVERYTHING WE OWN....

...AND THEY, AT LEAST, DIDN'T HAVE DAILY DEADLINES.

Often it takes a native New Yorker, such as Diana Wall, to notice the subtlest of changes in the city's atmosphere.

"I think this has to be a more receptive audience than during the Bicentennial year because the mood of the country is more patriotic than at that time," Wall said.

But that perception doesn't prevent her from being turned off by this event. "I think it's been appallingly over-commercialized around here on TV and by the newspapers, particularly the *New York Post,*" she said.

Couvares says there "seems to be a certain sense of excitement in the air — like things are about to pop. I noticed the buses are cleaner. I don't know if it's a coincidence or because of the Fourth celebration."

Drucker, who is 72, says he is fed up with promotions for the celebration.

"When you hear about the killing some of these people around here are making, it takes the spirit out of it for me," he said.

He tells of hearing about a restaurant in Brooklyn, expensive to begin with, that is raising its dinner prices to as much as $800 a meal. He also knows of people who own docks and cooperative apartments on the waterfront who are renting them to visitors for more than $1,000 for two or three days.

"In other words, it's a thing for the money people, ▶

WE'VE TRAVELED NEARLY 9,000 MILES IN THE LAST MONTH, BUT FINALLY DECIDED TO LEAVE THE DRIVING TO SOMEONE ELSE WHEN WE HIT NEW YORK CITY.
TAXI

which gives you a bad taste for the whole situation. If there was only more for people of moderate means, I'd appreciate it a little more," Drucker said.

"It looks like they're getting psyched up around here, that's for sure," said Joe Reddington of Queens. "Everyone seems to be coming in at the last minute. There's been lots of tourists the last couple of days."

Reddington claims that he can differentiate tourists from native New Yorkers without fail. More than the cameras around their necks and the baggage in their grasps, he says he can spot tourists because they're usually dressed in weekend wear in midtown Manhattan in the middle of the week.

"I see them looking up at the skyscrapers, and they start to get me looking up, too, like maybe there's something up there I haven't seen before," he said.

Unlike the other local residents, Reddington plans to witness the fireworks show firsthand Friday.

"I usually go to all the Fourth shows, but this one should really be amazing," he said. ∎

GREEN FOAM RUBBER LIBERTY CROWNS ARE BIG ON THE MANHATTAN STREETCORNERS AMONG PEDDLERS WHO OTHERWISE HAWK UMBRELLAS AND WINDUP TOYS.

MS. LIBERTY HERSELF SHOWED UP FOR THE FESTIVITIES AND HUNG OUT ON A PARK BENCH NEAR HERALD SQUARE HARANGUING PASSERSBY.

Day 2

Thousands of people from all over the world huddled on the chilly banks of New York Harbor. Many embraced and swayed as they sang "America the Beautiful" and watched the relighting of the Statue of Liberty.

Others were moved to tears as they gazed longingly at the statue that served as a symbol of freedom for so many millions of immigrants who entered the country through this port over the years.

"There she goes," someone cried out as a red glow shined on the statue's pedestal and a blue light moved slowly upward toward its torch. The cheers and applause from the Battery Park crowd rose in harmony with the bright white spotlights on the statue.

The renovated lady of liberty was radiant, the most brilliant light in the harbor.

"It's one of the most thrilling sights that I've ever seen. It's magnificent," said an emotional Mildred Schneider of Cranbury, N.J.

The relighting of the Statue of Liberty was meaningful for Schneider because five decades ago it stood as a sign of welcome to the United States for her parents and grandparents who came to the United States from Hungary.

Battery Park on the southern tip of Manhattan was the best vantage point to view the relighting ceremony for those who couldn't be on a boat in the harbor or who chose not to pay $10,000 for a ticket to Governor's Island to be with President Reagan and a host of dignitaries.

A tent was set up at the park with hundreds of chairs for watching the ceremonies on a bank of 14 television monitors. But nearly everyone picked up the chairs and moved them onto the lawn beside the harbor for an unobstructed view of the Liberty lighting. They felt as much a part of the ceremonies as the privileged few on Governor's Island.

A sense of warmth and brotherhood permeated the crowd. New York, often a frightening Oz for so many Americans, was now a welcome place. Throughout the night New York police were visible everywhere. It seemed as if the whole 27,000-member force was working the night shift. Maybe Mayor Koch was right, and New York really would be the safest city in the country this weekend.

The officers' biggest concern of the night appeared to be finding a van they towed by mistake that belonged to a disabled Vietnam War veteran visiting from Tennessee. The young man sat in his wheelchair outside a police trailer, wrapped in a blanket to ward off the cold and waiting for the embarrassed police to find his vehicle. For him, the night was ruined.

Earlier in the day, we had our first encounter with the throngs of visitors anticipated for the Fourth of July festivities. Masses of people were gathered at Manhattan's newly reconstructed South Street Seaport on the East River to watch a procession of "Small Ships" — a colorful flotilla of thousands of sloops, schooners, yachts and junks.

The weather was perfect — sunny, cool and breezy with a puffy cloud backdrop for the waves of photographers at the city's most scenic marina. Off the piers the small ships paraded south under the Brooklyn Bridge toward the Statue of Liberty as a prelude to the tall ships due to cruise up the Hudson River the next day.

Of all the boats that floated by the South Street Seaport, one always managed to capture the largest and loudest cheers from the viewers — a cruiser piloted by New York's finest, the city police department.

The crowd watching the small ships regatta was only a taste of what soon would arrive at the South Street district. By early afternoon the wide cobblestone walking malls were packed with hundreds of thousands of people.

The mood was festive, filled with laughter and chatter in an endless variety of accents and languages. It was a huge carnival. On each side of the walks, street vendors hawked Liberty Weekend wares: T-shirts, pennants, balloons, hats, posters, buttons, miniature statues and flags, bearing the unmistakable image of the Statue of Liberty or other patriotic themes.

But the most noticeable of all the souvenirs of the day were green foam rubber Statue of Liberty headdresses worn by thousands of children and adults alike. In many people's memories, the green crowns, more than anything else, will symbolize the patriotic mood of Liberty Weekend.

For $3 or two for $5, you, too, can look like the Statue of Liberty, was the sales pitch from every street corner.

"Yeah, they're selling like mad," said vendor John DeWitt.

"It's the lady's birthday," said his sister, Jeanie, "and they all want to be part of the celebration. It's fun, you know. I think they look kind of nice."

Another Liberty crown vendor, Stevie Clark, said he never expected such a demand.

"This is unbelievable. These things are going to be my ticket out of New York and back to the West Coast. I'm going for 500 a day — got to get out while I'm still standing," Clark said.

"This is what makes me feel like the spirit of the Fourth," said Mollie Butler of Brooklyn, appropriately wearing a Liberty crown. "But tomorrow, forget it. That's why we're here today."

Mary Allen, a native of Cincinnati who lives in Manhattan, took the Liberty costume a few steps ▸

LIBERTY-GREEN FLASHLIGHTS ARE ALL THE RAGE IN THE GRANDSTANDS, SELLING FOR EIGHT DOLLARS INCLUDING BATTERIES AND A YELLOW MOLDED PLASTIC FLAME.

WHEN INSTRUCTIONS FOR THE CROWD NEED TO BE STATED, THEY ARE GIVEN IN GRAND THEATRICAL FORM BY CLOWNS.

WHEN FESTIVITIES DRAG, THEY ALSO HELP THE CROWD FORGET THE STIFF CHILLING BREEZE COMING ACROSS THE WATER.

further. In addition to the green foam headdress, she tied her hair in a bun and draped herself in a flowing green gown so she looked like a lifesize version of the statue.

Her motivation, however, was not entirely patriotic. Although a nurse by trade, Allen considers herself an artist. She was selling black-and-white ink drawings of the statue for $1.50 each. By noon, she had sold one.

"I'm not your typical 'rah-rah' type of person, but I've always liked the Statue of Liberty. For me it has always symbolized the better part of America," Allen said.

Everyone knows New York's taxi cab drivers are smart. It should come as no surprise, then, that most of them picked what could be the busiest weekend in the city's history to go on strike.

An 8,000-member coalition of independent cabbies wanted more money and refused to work during the three-day celebration. The few hundred fleet-owned cabs that remained on the road commanded premium rates, often abandoning their meters for fares up to double the normal price. Twice, cabbies charged us $10 for rides that regularly would have been less than $5. Nevertheless, competition on the curbs was tough and an empty cab a rarity.

No myth about New York City took a bigger fall the last couple of days than the idea that all New Yorkers are crass, cold and unfriendly.

"All the people seem to be enjoying themselves more, and everybody seems to be a little friendlier," said Francois Hyterhoeven, who lives in Antwerp, Belgium.

In the short time Hyterhoeven has been here visiting his friend, Jack Heid, a former U.S. Olympic cyclist, he said, two instances stand out in his mind. He told of climbing aboard a New York City bus without the correct $1 in change. Two women opened their purses to help him.

Later, Hyterhoeven said, he was at a restaurant and having trouble deciding what to order. People who were sitting around him offered him tastes from their dinner plates.

"It's fantastic; it's the greatest celebration I've ever seen," Hyterhoeven said.

Michele Randall of Uptown Manhattan thinks the negative image outsiders have of New Yorkers has its roots in the makeup of the city.

"My basic philosophy is that this is a good city that works hard. A lot of tourists come in here, and they catch you in rush-rush situations," said Randall, a buoyant woman with big dimples who was selling "official" Liberty Weekend T-shirts.

"This is not an easy city to deal with. A lot of people come in here and misinterpret our attitudes. It's just a case of us not always having time to give directions, things like that."

If a visitor can't find a New Yorker to offer directions, there's always a variety of street signs to fall back on. But New York street signs aren't simple statements like "Don't Park" or "Merge." A sign in front of the New York City Public Library says "Don't Even Think About Parking Here." On Broadway a sign says "Fight Grid Lock (traffic jams) — Don't Block The Box (intersection)."

Some motorists have taken a cue by putting signs where you normally wouldn't expect them. One driver, not wanting to worry about thieves, parked his car in Central Park with a "No Radio" sign in the window.

A favorite New York pastime is star gazing. At the Palm Too steakhouse on Third Avenue, bartender Frank Stanley says he serves booze to all the big show business names. Warren Beatty is a regular, he said, often accompanied by Diane Keaton.

"I remember one night, if someone would have thrown a bomb in here, it would have knocked off half the biggest stars in the business. At one table sat Mick Jagger, Catherine Deneueve, Jack Nicholson and Kathleen Turner, and before the night ended, Donald Sutherland joined them.

"Last night Richard Gere was in here, and the night before (Yankees third baseman) Mike Pagliarulo," Stanley said.

APPLAUSE AND SINGING BREAK OUT SPONTANEOUSLY IN THE GRANDSTANDS.

Sure enough, before the night was over, who should come strutting in with a young woman on his arm but boxing promoter Don King, he of the long frizzy hair. He ate a lobster for dinner.

The stars don't come out only at night. Thursday morning, walking down a busy sidewalk on Park Avenue, we saw the elusive Jackie Onassis, dressed casually in a blue blouse and purple pants, sans sunglasses and carrying a briefcase.

If you hang around the entrance to the Dakota on any given day, you're likely to see conductor Leonard Bernstein, singer Roberta Flack, actress Lauren Bacall or John Lennon's widow, Yoko Ono, who all live at the exclusive Central Park cooperative.

"They're all very nice people and give very nice tips, especially at Christmas time," said Delfilm Hernaiz, the Dakota's doorman.

The excitement is everywhere for the big Fourth of July bash.

"I'm just as thrilled about this as I was when the Olympics came to Los Angeles," said Frances Kenny of Santa Monica, Calif.

Kenny, who is watching the small ships at the South Street Seaport, said she was not frightened by the prospect of being surrounded by 15 million people.

"There's nothing like being there. You can watch it on TV, but it's not the same. You can see pictures, but you can't touch it and feel it like you can here," she said.

Mary Massey of Chicago said, "It's much more 'up' here than it is back home. I'm really glad I'm here."

Some greater New York City residents have been caught up in the celebration, too. "It's fantastic, just great to live near a city where all of this is happening," said A.J. Castagnetta of suburban New Jersey. "You'll never see anything like this again. It's like being a part of history for me."

"People are getting ready to be wild, wearing all kinds of ridiculous things on their heads," said Ron Singer of Asheville, N.C., who came to the Liberty Weekend to promote a religious group he founded, In God We Trust Inc.

"Mirthfulness is not happiness. But I suspect a lot of these people will have a genuine good time, too," Singer said. ■

SOUTH STREET SEAPORT

JIM BORGMAN
NEW YORK CITY

118 NEW YORK

Day 3

Every red-blooded American loves a good fireworks show, and this one was supposed to be the best ever. Too bad the size and demeanor of the crowd probably ruined it for most people who had looked forward to watching it firsthand in South Manhattan.

Thousands of visitors who came to Battery Park July 4th expecting a cool, manageable crowd like the night before were shocked to find themselves swarmed under by the youth of the city.

Rather than work their way through the overwhelming, sometimes ugly, crowd, droves of people poured toward the uptown subway tunnels to escape the mob before the first firework had exploded. One New York police officer said the people jam might break up "about 4 a.m., if we're lucky."

It was a grim scene — more like a battle zone than a festival, with overturned trash cans, beer cans and bottles littering the streets. A stiff breeze blew dust and paper into the air. Bottle rockets and cherry bombs blew up every several seconds; boom boxes blasted music into the night; and the crowd moved in a crush to get past tall buildings for an unobstructed view of the fireworks. Tempers grew hot, but people only pushed harder.

Older people and parents with young children who came anticipating a glorious show were swallowed up by hooligans bent on raucousness. The glitter of the night before was tarnished, a dim memory.

Anyone who stuck it out was blasted on three sides by 10 tons of fireworks, but buildings blocked the view for most. It was impossible for anyone to see all of the fireworks except from a boat or aircraft.

"I think it's very rude of them to have this building going up in front of us," said Scottie Twine, who was with her husband, Jeff, on crowded Greenwich Street looking west toward the Hudson River. The Twines, from the Upper East Side, were able to ignore all the detracting factors to enjoy the show at least a little.

"There's something so magical about them you forget that they're man-made," she said.

Jeff Twine's theory was that most people who came to view the show probably just needed an excuse to get out of the house. "It's a release, you know. It's something different, the noise, the color; the vibration is exciting."

If the half-hour fireworks show was as good as Cincinnati's annual Riverfest show, few around Battery Park would have been able to notice.

The day began on an enjoyable, emotional pitch with no indication of what was to come. At Pier 86 on the Hudson River, with the Tall Ships of the world passing by in splendid, full-sail regalia, reality hits you like a stiff gust of ocean wind: We really are a nation populated primarily by immigrants.

Visitors from across the country line the west bank of Manhattan island to watch the ships. They share a common bond in their appreciation of a beautiful sight; they are united in their love of liberty. And for the second consecutive day, the weather is perfect, matching the smiles on most of the peoples' faces.

Something else everyone here has in common is that they or their ancestors originally came here from somewhere else, whether it was a bottom deck passage from Dublin or Liverpool, coach class from San Juan or Havana, or in chains from Nigeria.

Most of the people seem to be aware of their roots. Almost anyone could recite their family heritage and what this harbor means to them.

"When my grandfather got off the boat and they asked him his name, he said, 'Blablabla,' and that's how it came out," said Steve Koloskus of St. Louis, who watched the tall ships with his brother, Dan, of Columbus, Ohio.

"It's amazing how all these millions of people came through here not knowing the language or anyone who lived here. I just moved to St. Louis and didn't know anyone, and it's real hard, but nothing like what they had to go through," Steve Koloskus said.

The Koloskuses' grandfather who gave them their surname came through Ellis Island from Eastern Europe in 1914. Their other relatives arrived from Greece and Ireland.

Dan Koloskus said he regretted missing the Bicentennial celebration.

"I thought I'd never get a second chance, so I had to be here. I'm just delighted with all of this — I love sailing. It's better to be here than in Columbus saying, 'Oh, I missed it again.' I love it. I love New York," he said.

Steve Koloskus said, "You'd have to be a real cynic for this not to get to you."

As Steve Koloskus' flight arrived the previous evening, he said, all the passengers rushed to one side of the plane to see the newly refurbished Statue of Liberty. ▶

"It was unreal, so many boats in the harbor, and everyone on the left side of the plane. The stewardess was shouting in the microphone, 'Get back in your seats.' But everyone ignored her."

Michael Gay of Princeton, N.J., came to America from his native Haiti in 1965, just out of high school.

"Things were pretty bad there then, but I was probably too young to know the difference. I was just a high school kid living it up, too busy having fun to know what was going on in Haiti," said Gay, now a construction foreman, married and the father of three. His daughter, 12, and sons, 8 and 3, took turns on his shoulders to see the tall ships above the crowd.

As an immigrant, Gay said, the Statue of Liberty "means a lot to me. More than anything else, I think it's the ideal of what you're celebrating this weekend more than the actual presentation."

"I like the boats in the water, but that's about it," said Gay's sister-in-law, Tamara Bissainthe of Queens, also a Haitian immigrant, who was helping Gay care for his children.

"When I came here, I was happy to be here, but I don't remember much because I was only 7," she said. "I just think of it as a nice big statue out there."

Gay said that he was caught up in the spirit of the Liberty Weekend and that he saw a lot of the same signs in others.

"I guess this is more of a stimulating thing for people. More than anything else, it seems to bring people together; they're going out of their way to be more accommodating, at least for a couple of days, anyway."

Shoulders such as Gay's were among the most common observation spots for viewers of the tall ships. But almost everything was a potential vantage point. Other means of seeing over tall buildings and hairy heads were:
■ Atop wooden packing crates and milk cartons snatched from nearby wharf warehouses;
■ On overturned trash cans, ladders and concrete blocks;
■ From piers, parking decks and nearly every building on the shores of New Jersey, Brooklyn and Manhattan;
■ As aircraft passengers on blimps, planes and helicopters or seagoers on pleasure craft ranging from yachts to inflatable rafts, although to ride on the sightseeing boats you risked being loudly booed every time you passed another pier — "Get out of the way," the viewers yelled;

■ On the huge deck of the U.S. Navy aircraft carrier *Intrepid*, where a crowded barbeque was in full swing.

"My parents thought they'd have better opportunities here when they arrived from Italy in 1903," said Michael Volgarino, 76, who was dressed in a tweed cap, red scarf, jeans jacket and shorts on the 80-degree day.

"It was still a fairly new country then and opportunities were unlimited for a shoemaker like my father," he said.

Volgarino grew up one of 12 children in Mount Holly, N.J. Never once, he said, did he hear his parents speak Italian.

"We were raised as Americans, not Italians, and English is all I've ever known," he said. "It helped them to adapt very easily and very comfortably to life in America."

The traffic engineers of New York City earned their paychecks this week. Most motorists Friday heeded the warnings to avoid driving here, making the streets of Manhattan as clear as if it were 4 a.m. No doubt this delighted the few hundred cab drivers who weren't on strike: They drove as if they were running in the Monte Carlo.

Ohioans Terry Doty of Mount Healthy and Lisa Boone of Fairfield proved that a Liberty Weekend itinerary didn't require months of planning. They work for a car leasing company and drove in from Cincinnati the day before to deliver a car in New Jersey. On the spur of the moment, they decided to catch a view of the tall ships and later in the day take in the fireworks show.

"It's neat. Everyone's getting together here, all the tall ships and stuff. Now we're working on a little of the liberty spirit," Boone said, lifting a cool cup of beer to her mouth.

Plenty of derelicts still roamed the back streets of the city, but they were not aggressive or preying on the masses of tourists for handouts. A visitor had far more to fear from the working cabbies, who would empty your wallet faster than you could say "I love New York."

George Bernhard, an attorney from Columbus, Ohio, was enjoying the tall ships floating by. He said he wanted to see the fireworks, too, but he didn't have a ticket. He was hoping some earlier philanthropy might help him somehow.

"I contributed money to this Liberty effort and got a card from (Lee) Iacocca," he said, flashing a green-and-white plastic card in his wallet. "I hope I can at least get something good out of it."

Under a viaduct near the Hudson River piers, a group of Jamaicans played congas and marimbas to the delight of a large gathering. The scene characterized the jovial atmosphere of the day. People from different walks of life danced side-by-side, although not very well, in a style more like a square dance than a Latin rumba. Everyone pressed closer, laughing and clapping in unison, urging on the band and dancers.

If only they could have captured that same feeling to release later that night at Battery Park. ■

NEW YORK

Liberty Sketchbook

by JIM BORGMAN in NEW YORK CITY

"HEY, LIBERTY NECKLACES! GLOW IN THE DARK! CHECK IT OUT!"

THERE IS A TERRIFIC CHARGE OF COSMOPOLITAN ENERGY ON THE STREETS OF NEW YORK CITY. A VIRTUAL UNITED NATIONS WILL PASS BEFORE YOU ON ANY STREET CORNER IN TEN MINUTES' TIME.

Battery Park

AT THE SOUTHERN TIP OF MANHATTAN, IT'S THE BEST SEAT IN THE HOUSE.

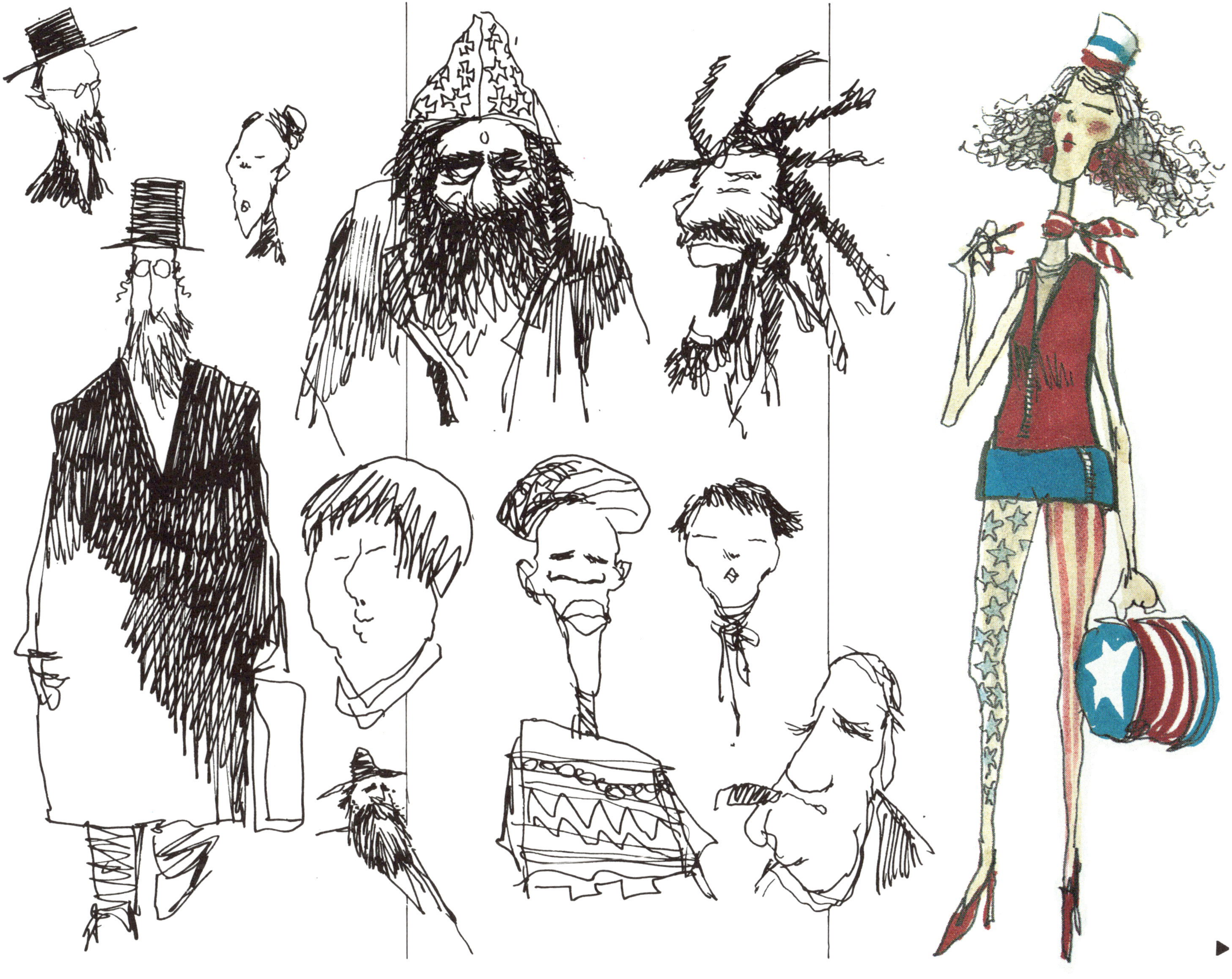

New York cab drivers alone bear testimony to the charisma of this country. Their job is rugged, the pay none too hot, but all — Haitians, Lebanese, Pakistanis, Kenyans — were struggling to stay. Olabi Zee showed me scars where he had been injured in the bombing of the American Embassy in Beirut. He was trapped in a tank under the rubble for two days. He had fired at the truck bomb as it approached. As a reward for his efforts he asked the U.S. Government for help getting into this country. He carries a certificate of commendation in his cab.

YES, THE COMMERCIALIZATION OF LADY LIBERTY IS EVERY BIT AS BAD AS YOU EXPECTED.

Overwhelming as New York can be even to an American, I walk these streets trying to imagine the courage it took to step off the boats at Ellis Island into this most foreign of foreign lands...

THE HOMELESS AND TEMPEST-TOST ARE STILL HERE, BESIDE THE GOLDEN DOOR.

Wrap-up

There's no place like home... There's no place like home...

Never again will I begrudge the parking garages downtown their four dollars a day............

Click click click

In Manhattan they charge $8.77 for the first hour.

As our 727 from LaGuardia Airport banked past downtown Cincinnati, I think we felt the kind of overwhelming emotion our ancestors experienced coming into New York Harbor past the Statue of Liberty.

It must have something to do with rejoining loved ones and seeing familiar sights. For us, it meant seeing our wives and families again instead of the procession of strangers we had grown to expect. After a month of gazing wide-eyed at strange skylines and terrain, it meant looking out the airplane window at local landmarks like the Carew Tower, Riverfront Stadium and Ault Park Pavilion.

So it must have been for the boatloads of immigrants laying eyes for the first time on the Statue of Liberty, for many a figure made familiar from years of studying photographs. Here she was at last, rising majestically before them, the ultimate symbol of welcome to the land of freedom.

Freedom is an intangible possession that we hold dear in our hearts, but often take for granted. The past month of June, 1986, and especially the past few days at the start of July, forever changed our attitudes in that respect.

One scene from among the 16 stops on our barnstorming journey across America keeps popping into our minds. It rises above the jumble of emotions and mental snapshots from a trip as intense as the one that just ended.

It is a mental picture of a 50-year-old black man in Tunica, Miss., named Elliseara Lowery. Everyone calls him "Sonny."

Lowery appears to be much older than his age. He grew up on a cotton plantation, worked his way up to being a field foreman and later learned to be a carpenter. He's basically retired now after suffering a few heart attacks. On the day we met him, he was sitting on a beat-up, wooden chair under a willow tree in his side yard, wiling away the hours on a 102-degree day.

"I don't have nothing else to do all day except sit right here in the shade," Lowery said.

He offered us a seat on a broken down air-conditioner; then he opened himself up to us — a couple of white Yankee strangers — baring his

128 LIBERTY

"I HAVE ALWAYS RELIED ON THE KINDNESS OF STRANGERS,...."

SAYS BLANCHE DUBOIS IN 'A STREETCAR NAMED DESIRE' AND SO, TOO, HAVE WE ON THIS TRIP ACROSS AMERICA.

WE'VE ASKED PEOPLE FOR DIRECTIONS. WE'VE ASKED THEM TO SHARE THEIR DEEPEST FEELINGS. THEY'VE OFFERED TO DRIVE US AROUND TOWN, MAIL OUR MAIL, ANSWER EVERY QUESTION WE'VE HAD ABOUT THEIR THOUGHTS.

AMERICA IS AN IRREPRESIBLY FRIENDLY COUNTRY. AMERICANS ARE BIG-HEARTED PEOPLE.

innermost thoughts, his past fears and his hopes for the future. Later, he even suggested that we take a driving tour with him of Tunica County, the poorest county in the United States.

Lowery's pride and joy in this world is his house, a wood-sided, red-painted, one-story dwelling that most people would consider no more than a step above a shack. But to Lowery, this home, built with his own hands, might as well be Graceland Mansion, which is up the road about 30 miles in Memphis, Tenn.

He started the building project by ordering floor plans for $10 from *Popular Mechanics* magazine, and whether it was a sunny or rainy day, he pounded nails into the frame of his humble abode. It took him five years to finish. He borrowed a little money from the bank to get started, and when that ran out, he worked for a while to pay the loan back, then returned to the bank to borrow a little bit more.

"That was the only way they'd do it for me," Lowery said.

If anyone had a good reason to feel cheated by life, vindictive for being let down by the government or demoralized by discrimination from the wealthy, it was Lowery. But he was the most optimistic person we ▶

LIBERTY 129

Nell Surber take note:

AFTER WATCHING A LOT OF AMERICAN CITIES TICK, WE'VE CONCLUDED THAT CINCINNATI IS NO MORE THAN A GOOD SANDY BEACH AND A SMALL MOUNTAIN RANGE AWAY FROM PUTTING IT ALL TOGETHER.

met in our travels, typical, really, of a breed of people we found everywhere. There were other admirable souls:

David Borge, a young fisherman from Gloucester, Mass., who welcomed us onto his fishing trawler, and although he had not seen his wife and children for five days, took an hour of his time to show us the different gauges and compartments on the boat and explain what it's like to live on the ocean.

Johnny Humphreys, 77, Dixon, Ill., who delighted in retelling little secrets from President Reagan's past and told of his weekly calls to the White House to keep the president informed of goings on in his hometown.

Royal Andrews, an innkeeper in Packwood, Wash., near Mount St. Helens, who claimed to drink a half-case of beer every night and who feuded with Harry Truman over the price he charged for beers years before Truman became a celebrity and was covered under 300 feet of ash.

All of these were the ordinary people we found who make up the framework of our country, not well-spoken Chamber of Commerce types whose job it is to paint attractive pictures of a region or highly paid celebrities who try hard to look pretty and impress visiting newspaper reporters.

Did these people turn on the charm for us because we work for a newspaper? We don't think so. We rarely approached anyone by saying, "Hi, we're from *The Cincinnati Enquirer* . . ." Rather, we spoke with them as any stranger would. Usually, they were as open and friendly as if we had known them for years.

Even in the subways of New York City, a chamber of horrors for many out-of-towners, people were cordial, often starting up a conversation or lending a hand with directions through the underground maze. For the week of the Liberty celebration at least, New York was a very enjoyable place.

We couldn't look into people's minds; we didn't know whether they were thinking "what a couple of jerks" or something worse. But it's pretty easy to read people's eyes, and most looked genuine.

If there was a dominant impression we received around the country, it was of open arms and helpfulness. The United States is a big-hearted country that still admits more immigrants each year than the rest of the nations of the world combined. Sure, people are outspoken in their criticism of the way the affairs of the nation are handled, but even public outcries have to be taken in the proper context. We're in a league by ourselves — it's tough competing with the best.

A good example of that is Dixon, where many of the residents feel let down by their native son's economic policies. But are they marching the streets, campaigning against Reagan, destroying all evidence that he ever lived here? Nope, they're fixing up his boyhood home on South Hennepin Street, and they celebrated the Fourth of July weekend with their annual Petunia Festival.

Everywhere we visited, people are feeling prosperous at the same time they break their backs to make a living. They're happy at the same time the hardships of others make them sad; they're optimistic at the same time the forces of business and nature make it difficult to improve their lot in life.

How can this be? It must be human nature; people are basically good. When you see so many different segments of society and speak to so many people, it's difficult to imagine random, unprovoked violence. We felt that in the back alleys of New York City, along the wretched shacks of the Sugar Ditch in Tunica and on the boardwalk of Venice Beach, Calif., where hopeless drug addicts on a track toward destruction were all around us. Maybe we were just lucky, but they always stayed to themselves.

The uniformity of Americans also amazed us. Whether we were in the Pacific Northwest, the Rocky Mountains, the Southwest, Midwest, Mideast or South, it didn't make any difference — everyone we encountered could speak the same language; everyone was concerned and helpful and informed about the affairs of the region and much of the country. Most of these people have opinions on the way things should be and aren't bashful about sharing them.

A lot of this has to do with our excellent communication and transportation systems. Although a resident of one region of countries such as China, Italy or the Soviet Union might not be able to understand a fellow countryman speaking one of many dialects, Americans can speak with most anyone in the country and have nothing to worry about except dueling accents.

We were spoiled, too, by the ease of traveling around the country. One morning we were in Cincinnati, a few hours later we stood at the base of Mount St. Helens.

What is the mood of America? It is people's confidence in their abilities to earn a good living, whether taming bucking broncos in Fort Worth, Texas, or grinding horseradish in Lancaster, Pa.; it is a feeling of pride in hometowns, whether in a neighborhood of air-conditioned adobe haciendas in Sun City, Ariz., or among cool mountain chalets in Salt Lake City, Utah; it is a love of freedom to do whatever they want to for fun, whether catching alligators in the Florida Everglades or straddling a greasy pole suspended over the ocean in Gloucester, Mass.

Fifty separate states, one united country, and a wide diversity of people are, we found, what makes it great. ■

COMING SOON: The Mood of the Bahamas '86

by JIM BORGMAN and James F. McCarty

LIBERTY 133

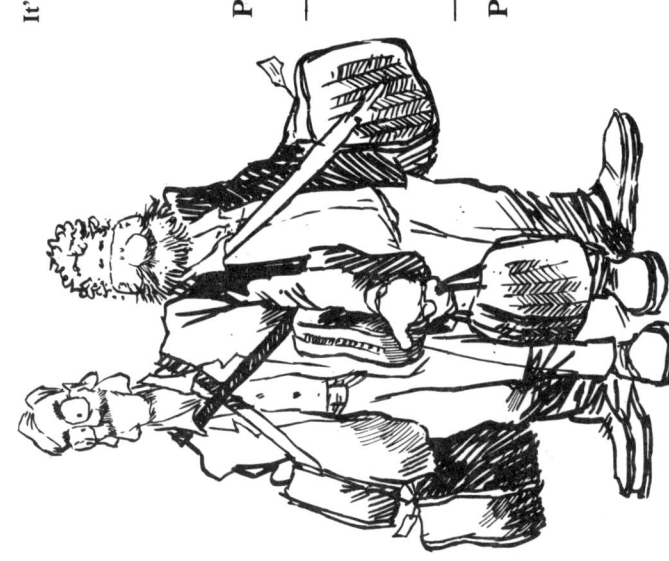

It's easy to order extra copies of *The Mood of America* - just remove this form, fill it out and

Mail to: The Cincinnati Enquirer
The Mood of America
P.O. Box 239
Cincinnati, Ohio 45202

Please send me:

_____ copies of *The Mood of America* at $10.95 _____
Add $.60 per copy Ohio sales tax _____
Postage and handling per book, $1.50 _____

Total: _____

Please send to: _____
Name (please print)

_____
Address

_____   _____   _____
City   State   Zip

Allow 3-4 weeks delivery   (Enclose check or money order)

It's easy to order extra copies of *The Mood of America* - just remove this form, fill it out and

Mail to: The Cincinnati Enquirer
The Mood of America
P.O. Box 239
Cincinnati, Ohio 45202

Please send me:

_____ copies of *The Mood of America* at $10.95 _____
Add $.60 per copy Ohio sales tax _____
Postage and handling per book, $1.50 _____

Total: _____

Please send to: _____
Name (please print)

_____
Address

_____   _____   _____
City   State   Zip

Allow 3-4 weeks delivery   (Enclose check or money order)